WALKING AGAIN

JUSTIN P. LANE

Walking Again

Copyright © 2019 by Justin P. Lane

Published by Tactical 16, LLC.

Colorado Springs, CO

ISBN: 978-1-943226-37-5 (paperback)

Printed in the United States of America

This is dedicated to all the servicemen and women who have sacrificed for the American freedom we have today, and to all my family who have been by my side since July 2, 2011.

May God bless each and every one of you!

CONTENTS

ACKNOWLEDGMENTS

First, I give all the glory to God for giving me purpose to continue living this life. Second, I would like to thank my wife, Crystal, for helping me become a better man each day. Lastly, I would like to thank my dad for guiding me to be the man I am today.

FOREWORD

Throughout our lives we run into negative people. They tell us who we're supposed to be, how we're supposed to act, what we can and can't do, and the rules we're supposed to conform to. Many people simply follow that path of complacency and lead a life of normality, never challenging what they hear or what they see. But not everyone follows that path.

This story is about one man who chose not to listen to those voices of conformity and doubt—a man who chose not to believe the limitations the doctors and therapists had set for him—one man who chose to put his trust in God.

This is the story of Justin "JP" Lane.

In the Army, he learned to never accept defeat and to never surrender.

And he never has...

— *Crystal Lane*

1

THE UNEXPECTED

At Birth

Kids grow up hearing stories about themselves that stick with them their entire lives—stories that parents tell over and over until they are cemented into their children's minds. For me, one of those stories was the night my brother and I snuck out of bed for a midnight snack. I was about six years old and my brother, Anthony, was maybe five, and we took almost everything off the refrigerator and pantry shelves that we could reach. We had a high time sampling crackers, lunchmeat, and Little Debbie snack cakes. The kitchen floor was covered in flour, cereal and ketchup. Imagine the surprise on our parents' faces the next morning when they found their two little boys covered in peanut butter and powdered sugar.

But the one childhood story that has stuck with me over the years is the story of my birth. It was the single most important story of my childhood that my father consistently retold to me. I was welcomed into the world five weeks ahead of my due date on May 30, 1988. I was a preemie, weighing in at just five pounds and six ounces.

Most newborn babies seem fragile and delicate, but my dad told me I was strong. He said I lifted my head and held it up. Even the attending doctor said to my dad, "He will be a strong boy." Neither of them could know at that moment just how true their words would turn out to be.

As my parents held me in their arms, smiling and cooing at their wiggly baby with bright blue eyes, they could never have imagined what my life would look like only twenty-three short years later.

But we can't jump to the future just yet. Every story has its beginning....

* * *

My parents met at church and got married in December of 1987 at a chapel on the Air Force base where my dad was stationed. I was welcomed into the world soon after, followed by my little brother, Anthony. My two oldest siblings, Sacha and Erik, were from my dad's first marriage. Sacha is a lovely woman, but as a child, it seemed her mission in life was to be the biggest bully possible to her siblings. My half-brother Erik could always get me laughing, no matter what kind of mood I was in. Sure, we fought just like any other siblings, but we never doubted our love for one another. Arguments and discord were part of our daily lives, but with maturity came love and a mutual respect. I have two older half siblings from my mother's side as well—Ariann and Jacob. My stepbrother Eric and my stepsister Gina came into my life later on when my dad married Kristi, the love of his life.

But in the late 1980's, my dad was still in the Air Force and my mom was a teacher; we moved around so much that it's difficult to even remember which house is the setting for the beginning of my story. We were always on the go, from a farm home to an inner-city block, from a trailer home to a red brick bed and breakfast. It was far from an idyllic hearts-and-roses family.

Like many of my childhood peers, my parents divorced when I was young, and I was brought up in a broken home.

Anthony, Ariann, Jacob and I lived together for a while in Marietta, Ohio until my parents' marriage started to suffer. They divorced when I was eight. Anthony and I were told we would be living with my mom, who had won custody. I still vividly remember sitting on the front porch, my hands in my lap and tears on my cheeks, asking my dad, "Why can't

I go with you?" I sat watching the dust settle in the driveway as he drove away. My young heart and mind were not equipped to deal with the pain and hurt that soon headed my way.

We moved even more now with just my mother, and it seemed each new house came with a new boyfriend. She took care of kids all day as a teacher, so I felt like the last thing she wanted to do was come home from work to take care of four more. Needless to say, we had a lot of Chef Boyardee Ravioli and Hamburger Helper meals.

I didn't feel like Anthony and I were a priority in her life—she always had other things to do. I would even take cash from her purse to make sure my little brother had lunch money for school. I was thrust into what felt like an early adulthood, raising my younger brother and learning to provide for myself.

Anthony and I always had an escape plan to run away... but we never put that plan into action. We both wanted to live with our dad and couldn't understand why we only got to visit him in the summer and sometimes at Christmas. We found solace in being together, listening to music.

We enjoyed all genres: hip hop, country, Christian, pop—pretty much anything on the radio. When we visited my dad, we would dig through all his CDs looking for new songs to jam out to. I found myself beating out drum rhythms on the car dash or the kitchen table, much to my father's consternation. My dad was a whiz on the guitar, and he would play and sing country songs for us after dinner. Those were the best days: just being in my dad's incredible presence, listening to him sing and pick the guitar. He was an inspiration. He taught me a few chords, but I gravitated more toward percussion.

I was twelve when I found out that on my next birthday I could choose which parent I wanted to live with. My dad was living in Green Bay, Wisconsin at the time and we were definitely ready for a change of scenery. As soon as I became a teenager, Anthony and I packed our bags and we were out of there!

My dad drove down to get us, and we took a ten-hour road trip across the country in his 1994 Isuzu Rodeo. I distinctly remember a gas station with a McDonald's in an enclosed walkway where we stopped to eat, and all of us arguing what tunes we were going to listen to next. We made several visits to rest stops for dad to take power naps to keep us safe on the road.

The weekend we arrived in Green Bay, he took us to the youth retreat taking place at the church he attended, Spring Lake Church. We were a little taken aback, hoping we would get to soak up more time with the dad we had been missing, but were still happy to go.

It was years later when my dad told me, "I knew you would both need Jesus, and I knew I would need a break from you two after a ten-hour car ride!" That little "break" was actually a blessing that my heart and soul needed. That weekend of the church retreat was when the seed was planted in my heart that would grow into my yearning to know Jesus.

* * *

The Day the World Stopped Turning

It was during my eighth-grade year at Lombardi Middle School in Green Bay when two very unexpected events took place in my life.

The first came two months after we had moved in with my dad. My mom drove to our home, packed Anthony's things, and took him away from us. She didn't care about what he wanted, but only reasoned that although *I* may be old enough to legally choose who I wanted to live with, Anthony was not, something she had just found out. She took my only full-blood sibling away from me that day. I had no idea what was going to happen to him back in Ohio.

Anthony did finally make his way back to us a little over a year later. I remember him being a little different, distant even; the time we spent apart was more like a chasm than a year. But it was so good to have my brother back. Our little family felt complete once more. Sure, we still fought like all brothers do, but when it came down to it, we knew we always had each other's back, no matter what. It took me many years and the support of my wife, Crystal, to finally bring forgiveness into the relationship I have with my mom because she separated me and my brother.

The second event of my eighth-grade year that changed the course of my life was the terrorist attacks of September 11, 2001.

Every generation has a day that is simply unforgettable. Some will always remember what they were doing when Pearl Harbor was attacked, others remember the assassination of John F. Kennedy, and some remember watching the television as the space shuttle Challenger exploded. For my generation, it's 9/11.

Everyone can tell you where they were when they heard about the first plane flying into the north tower of the World Trade Center—what they were doing, who they were with and how their entire day was spent afterward. I was sitting in my literature class when the teacher abruptly stood up from her desk and walked out of the classroom. My classmates and I were a little confused, but pleasantly surprised when she came back in wheeling a television. "Yes! Movie time," I thought to myself.

She plugged it in and tuned to a news station, and we saw a wide-angle shot of smoke billowing out of the first tower. Minutes later we watched in horror as the second plane crashed into the south tower. Everyone in the class was in tears.

"We are being attacked," we were told. "War will soon start." It was at that very moment that I knew as soon as I was old enough, I would be joining the military to fight for my country.

* * *

My Adolescence

MY TEENAGE YEARS CAME WITH THE TYPICAL TEENAGE distractions: school, sports, cars, friends, garage bands and girls. I sang in the choir at school and played drums in the worship band at church. Some buddies from church and I formed a rock band. We changed the name of it so many times that I cannot remember what we called ourselves. I played drums, of course, and was pretty good at it, if I say so myself.

During my senior year I fell in love with a foreign exchange student from Mexico. We were inseparable for the entire year, and after graduation I followed my high school sweetheart to Mexico. We would eventually marry before my deployment.

While in Mexico, I had completely forgotten about the promise I made myself when I was only thirteen. Then one life-changing day, Anthony called and told me he wanted to join the Army. His declaration jolted my memory and took me back to that terrible day in my eighth-grade literature class when the twin towers came crashing down in a heap of metal and dust. I saw this moment as God's way of giving me a little shove toward my life's purpose.

I left Mexico soon after and met Anthony back home in Green Bay. We didn't tell our dad about our plan, but we were both bubbling with excitement at the thought of going to the recruitment office the next morning. My mind was racing with thoughts and questions, and I couldn't get to sleep. What did my future hold? When would I go to war? What would dad think? Morning seemed to come quite quickly, and when my alarm buzzed, I was up and dressed in five minutes.

I walked down the hall to Anthony's bedroom and exclaimed, "Wake up! Time to go sign that dotted line!"

Although Anthony will argue a different version of this story, I remember him groggily mumbling, "I changed my mind. I'm going to college and save up to buy a Chrysler Crossfire."

I laughed at his sudden change of plans and interest in one certain vehicle... a plan so specific!

I said, "All right, man, but I'm still doing it!"

So in September of 2008, with my heart pounding out of my chest, I got in the car and headed downtown to the recruitment offices. My hands were shaking with anticipation as I pulled into the parking lot and found an empty space. I knew my life was about to change and would never be the same again. I was beginning a new chapter. I stood in front of the imposing building, reading the signs for the different branches plastered across each door. I remembered Anthony saying he wanted to join the Army, so I took a deep breath, pushed the door open and stepped inside.

A recruiter dressed in his fancy green uniform stepped up to greet me. "How can I help you?" he asked.

"I am here to join the Army," I firmly stated. "What is currently the most dangerous job?"

Without missing a beat, he said "Twelve Bravo, Combat Engineer."

I raised my hand to shake his. "Great. Sign me up," I said enthusiastically.

Having not told my dad where I was going, I knew a tough conversation awaited me at home. If I remember correctly, he didn't speak to me for an entire week, which seemed like an eternity because we had always been so close.

First and foremost, he thought I should have joined the Air Force and followed in his footsteps. Secondly, I had signed up for a very dangerous position which, of course, would not sit well with any parent. While he was certainly not happy with me, he eventually did what all good parents do—forgive, love and support their children, no matter how crazy their choices may seem. He understood that I had to follow my own path and he would support me in my decision, even if he didn't agree with it one hundred percent.

2

ARMY BOUND

Basic Training

The rest of the recruits and I stepped off a plane and straight onto a bus. As soon as I parked myself in an empty seat, the drill sergeant's loud voice boomed over the crowd, "Sit down, shut up, and keep your heads covered. If any one of you should lift your head to see where we are going, so help me, I will shove my boot so far up your..."

You get the idea.

I later heard that they didn't want you to see the location of the base in hopes that you wouldn't be able to find your way out if you decided to give it a try. Soon the bus came to a stop, and I knew the verbal onslaught would be coming again. But I was ready for this. I was BORN for this. And soon, my body and my mind would be built for this.

I took one step off the bus into the warm greetings of, "Get off my bus!" and "Who do you think you are, son?!" and "You ain't *nothing* until I'm done with you!" The shouts came from every direction as drill sergeants lined up for a verbal beatdown of their fresh, green recruits. Life was about to get rough.

We were constantly reminded that though our enlistment papers listed Private or Private First Class for our ranks, we were not soldiers until we completed our training. We dumped out our civilian bags, turned in our phones and other personal items, and began physical training. PT was a physically brutal and mentally demanding experience designed to break us down, make us weak and increase our desire to give up.

But I am a Lane... and I knew I would not be giving up. Right then and there, on day one, surrounded by the men who would either quickly wash out or go on to be someone extraordinary, I gave myself a little pep talk: "Three and a half months of my superiors yelling at me, the hardest physical labor I'd ever endured, and... shooting things? Yea... I got this!" I knew *exactly* why I had joined the Army and I couldn't wait to get out there and fight for my country.

I ran track in high school, but only short distances, so going from running 200 meters to running two to five miles every few days was not an easy feat. Add on the fact that these runs began at 5:00 a.m. and it made for unenjoyable mornings to say the least. I felt like Forrest Gump: I just kept running and running and running. Remembering my lack of energy and enthusiasm on these pre-dawn runs still makes me chuckle to myself.

My days were packed not only with physical activity, but with a wide variety of educational experiences. We covered quite a few topics in Basic Combat Training and Advanced Individual Training (AIT): how to shoot our rifles, how to quickly disassemble and reassemble our firearms, how to navigate and how to survive in the wilderness.

During basic, some of the recruits were given leadership responsibilities by the drill sergeants, anything from squad leaders to platoon leaders. I was given the responsibility to lead my platoon, and I surprised the drill sergeants with how well I performed. I made sure my troops were on time, geared up and in tight formation.

One memory that has really stuck with me through the years was when one of my soldiers didn't perform a task as required. Anyone who knows anything about basic training knows that it isn't the individual soldier who is punished for a mistake, it's the rest of the platoon. That soldier has to stand by and watch his brothers-in-arms work out a punishment for his "crime." So, after we got back to the barracks, my squad leaders and I thought he needed a punishment as well.

We decided he would have a double shift on night guard duty. I let him know about his new assignment, and he was pretty irritated. His attitude led to an argument that turned into a fight. Keep in mind, I didn't have a strong walk in my Christian faith yet. I was a platoon leader and, at least temporarily, I was someone's superior; that someone was talking back to me.

I won't go into all the details of that conversation, but I am pretty sure he woke up with a sore jaw the next morning. He did have the respect to approach me later, offer an apology for his disobedience, and we parted on good terms. I still have a high regard for him to this day. It takes a strong man to admit when he is wrong, especially in the Army.

My leadership ended after a month or so. I found out later from one of the drill sergeants that I was doing too good of a job at keeping my men in line. They put the worst soldier in charge of the platoon to ensure more mess ups, therefore, more physical training for us. Apparently, we all needed our butts kicked around a little more.

The two most important lessons that came out of my basic training experience were to adopt a strict personal discipline and to develop a fighting spirit that would never allow me to give up or surrender. I didn't know it then, but those two lessons prepared me for what awaited in the future.

At the time, I thought I was living through fourteen weeks of hell, but now, looking back with the knowledge and experience I have under my belt today, it could have been considered heaven. What was to come in my life would create an entirely new definition of what I knew to be hell.

* * *

After Training

AS TRAINING WAS COMING TO AN END, I FOUND OUT I WOULD BE reporting to the 428th Engineer Company stationed in Wausau, Wisconsin. As an Army Reservist, I trained one weekend a month, allowing time for work or continued schooling. The idea was to do my eight-year contract with the Army in the Reserve then move on to full-time active duty to pursue a career in Special Forces.

With this in mind, I was ready to get back to Mexico. I wrote up my proposal and it was passed up the chain of command for approval. Much to my surprise, it came back stamped "Approved" before our weekend drills were completed. This allowed me to move to Mexico to be with my girlfriend and come back to Wausau to train with my troops on a quarterly basis.

I settled into Puebla, Mexico with Nadia, who was in college to become a massage therapist. Right away I started looking for a job to keep me busy. Since English is my native language, I figured that I could teach. I visited a couple of schools and soon found an elementary school that hired me. The principal instructed me to speak only English with the children to immerse them in the language. I was allowed to translate into Spanish if they truly couldn't understand what I was trying to say.

What kept the job interesting was that I didn't speak much Spanish. As the days marched forward, I was learning just as much Spanish from the kids as they were learning English from me. One memorable student still sticks out in my mind today. He had a difficult time understanding me and following along in English, more so than most, so it was hard for him to stay engaged and interested. This led to many naps in my class.

This kid would literally have his face planted flat on his desk, mouth hanging open, drool seeping from his lips. He had a sweet tooth, so I devised a plan to keep him awake...little powdered donuts. If he could stay awake for the entire class period, I would reward him with a donut at the end of class. This became quite an expensive way to teach, because I couldn't just buy one student donuts, I had to buy them for the whole class on a regular basis.

We were about midway through the school year when the principal came to me with a proposal. An English teacher at the middle school was moving, leaving an empty spot to fill. They asked if I could tackle my usual morning classes at the elementary school then head over to the middle school for three classes in the afternoon. I accepted and began my new classes right away.

As we crept forward to the end of the school year, the principals at both schools knew that I was a soldier and there was always a possibility that I would be called up for deployment. When it finally happened, it was—naturally—at an inopportune moment. I was prepping all my classes for final exams when the call came in that I was to deploy to Afghanistan.

Finally, in August of 2010, the day I had been waiting for arrived. Two full years after I had enlisted in the Army, the moment I was waiting for was here.

Nadia and I were at home, sitting on the couch and watching television. The phone rang and she got up to answer it. After she said hello, I saw a brief look of confusion on her face.

She held the phone out in my direction. "Someone needs to talk to you," she said.

I assumed it was my dad since no one else really ever called me here. A deep voice on the other end identified himself as the 428 Unit Administrator, Mr. Thomas St. John.

He started, "Lane, we need you to come back to the States."

I couldn't believe what I was hearing. "It's time. The unit is about to deploy. There is a plane ticket to Green Bay waiting on you," he said.

I could see Nadia out of the corner of my eye, waiting to hear whatever news was being delivered on the other end. But I could barely contain my excitement. Others might have dreaded getting a call like this, but I was ecstatic.

"Where are we going?" I asked.

"Afghanistan," he replied, "and it's gonna be hot."

We finished up our conversation and I told St. John, "See you soon."

The confusion on Nadia's face spread. My heart was beating out of my chest as I rested the phone back on the cradle.

"Where are you going?" she asked, rising from her position on the couch.

"That was my unit administrator. I have to go back to Green Bay," I explained. "We are going to be deployed." I swallowed hard, looking her in the eye. "To Afghanistan," I finished.

She burst into tears and I held her up, cradling her in my arms. This was the call she had feared since the moment we met. I promised her it would all be okay, and I would come back to her.

Her family surrounded us, showed support, and tried to help her cope with my sudden departure. No matter what country you live in, being called to deploy translates the same across nations and languages. It has the same effect on everyone's family: sadness, fear, worry, thoughts of their loved ones never returning home. There is no master plan you can follow for what might come next. I was about to leave my family and friends and go it alone.

As excited as I was to finally be called into action, I was deeply saddened to leave my life behind. I didn't even get the chance to write out the final exams for my students. I had to pack up and leave immediately. It tore me apart to leave all the kids I'd spent the entire year with, watching them grow and learn proper English. I wished I had time to finish out the year, but my duty to my country came first.

Because I had to leave so quickly, I didn't get a chance to say goodbye. I assume the principals told them I was called to fight. I couldn't bear the thought of them thinking that I had abandoned them. I often wonder what the kids thought had happened to me.

Do they assume I died? Served my time and went home? I never saw my students again. Sometimes I wonder if the principals and teachers would still be there if I went back to visit. The school was so remote, and things often change quickly in Mexico... I'm not sure I would even be able to find it if I tried.

3

BOOTS ON THE GROUND

Afghanistan! I was THRILLED. I couldn't wait to step off the plane and onto that Middle Eastern sand, but it's not a quick process to ship off to war.

Back in Wisconsin, we underwent an intense month of training for the job we were tasked to carry out. We were about to go from being soldiers walking around wearing uniforms saying, "Yup, we're soldiers," to being soldiers who knew how to protect their teammates, notice what others missed and potentially save the lives of others. We were going to learn what we needed to do in order to make it back home safely.

Lives were at stake—lives that depended upon me and my platoon doing a job well done. We learned how to make bombs, maneuver in vehicles designed to locate improvised explosive devices (IEDs), accurately hit our targets and work together to eliminate the enemy.

In the days before I left, Nadia flew up from Mexico to see me one last time. After about two years together, we decided to get married secretly in the courthouse. I would soon be kissing my new wife goodbye and heading overseas.

The 428th Engineer Company passed its training with flying colors and we deployed soon after. We consisted of three combat engineering platoons and a maintenance platoon responsible for the vehicles and equipment, about 120 troops total.

Everything we learned was soon to be put to the test, more than any of us could have imagined. We flew for days, stopping in two countries I'd never seen before, Ireland and Germany, to refuel and let the pilots rest up. One moment that stuck with me took place in the airport in Ireland. There was a beautiful civilian woman waiting on her flight. Everyone in my unit couldn't stop staring at her, but no one had the guts to walk up to her and say hello.

Everyone began taking bets and daring each other to go talk to her, but there weren't any takers. I was a newlywed, so I wasn't about to hit on her, but I couldn't pass up the chance to win a bet and show up the other men in my unit. So, I waltzed over to her, introduced myself and learned she was from Bolivia and headed home to see her family. I don't remember her name and never saw her again, but I relished in the fact that I took a dare no one else would.

Our stay at the U.S. base in Germany lasted about a week. We saw daily flights of small groups of soldiers flying into Afghanistan to relieve others that were going home. While I was growing more and more impatient to get over and join the fight, I was having a blast wandering around the base.

It was almost surreal to meet all these different soldiers from so many different countries who were all joining together for a single cause, to rid the world of its biggest evil. We taught each other a few words from our native languages and exchanged currencies as souvenirs. I still have some of it to this day.

It was an eye-opening experience to feel that drive, that NEED, to band together with brothers from all over the world to stop the terrorists that brought down our twin towers and that were still bringing untold horrors to the back doors of so many.

Word finally came down that my group would be the next to leave for Afghanistan. We packed up and loaded out in a Lockheed C-130 Hercules, a typical military transport aircraft. We were packed in like sardines, soldier after soldier, with all of our gear crammed into the belly of the plane. It was *exactly* as uncomfortable as it looks in the movies, and just as exciting, too.

We began a combat landing as we came into Kandahar, Afghanistan, which is done any time there is believed to be enemies in the area. A combat landing is designed to avoid giving any possible enemy presence an easy target. This is *every bit* as cool as it sounds! We twisted to the left, then rocked to the right, then dove to the ground in a corkscrew before leveling out with incredible precision and stopping on a dime. The lucky ones don't puke up their lunch and the ones that do get ragged on, but everyone walks off that plane feeling more alive than ever. No one ever forgets their first combat landing.

We gathered our gear as the back of the plane dropped down, and we all walked off feeling like heroes stepping out of a slow-motion scene in a war movie. We were quickly slapped back to reality as the plane door closed and a 120-degree sandstorm punched us in the face. This wasn't Green Bay, Wisconsin anymore. This was brutal and hot and dangerous.

This was Afghanistan. And it was time to get to work.

* * *

FOB Wilson

FORWARD OPERATING BASE (FOB) WILSON WAS TO BE MY HOME for the next eleven months. It housed thousands of troops, contractors and Afghan military personnel, all working together to keep the Kandahar Province safe. Each year a new division took command, and at the time of my duty, the 101st Airborne Division was leading our fight.

We were assigned tents and went to unpack. The soldiers we were to replace were busy packing their things to head home and were more than happy to leave some of their small luxuries behind, like mini fridges or cables, but only for a price. If we wanted any of these items to stay in our spots, we had to buy them. Not a bad little gig as long as you had cash, but even if you didn't, you could make a quick trip to the finance office, which was little more than a small room with an ATM.

We set up our own living spaces, which came with a bunk bed in each. The easiest way to work the setup was to toss all your gear on the top bunk and sleep on the bottom, but I remember one guy who insisted on sleeping on the top bunk. Every morning, he'd have to sleepily jump off the top and land on the floor below to prepare for our missions.

We were given a couple of days to get squared away and settled in before we had to roll out on our first convoy, so I used my time to build a small desk out of scrap wood. Soon I had a little place to eat and set up some of my electronics. It wasn't even close to the size of a college dorm room, but it was my home for now. I knew we had electricity off and on so you could say the proverbial light bulb went off above my head, both figuratively and literally. As the weeks went by, eating the same food every day, I came up with an amazing idea: I bought a pizza oven online and had it shipped to my base.

I asked my dad to send me some pizza sauce, pepperoni and grade A Wisconsin cheese for a little taste of home. I bought local bread in town and soon the guys and I were cooking up hot and cheesy pies right there in the tent. Pizza night at Casa de Lane became quite popular among my brothers-in-arms and it was nice to avoid the chow hall for the same old meals.

A few of the departing soldiers stayed behind to show us the ropes, taking us along the normal routes and introducing us to the areas we would be patrolling.

Fortunately it was winter, and the fighting season always calmed during that time, so it proved an easy task to get us familiar with the terrain. We didn't run into any issues, and we were fast learners, which allowed the soldiers going home to get out sooner, for which they were thankful. Before long, we were on our own clearing the paths for the convoys coming behind us, which could be anything from food and supply trucks to troop transports and vehicles heading out to clear a specific area of IEDs.

Every convoy that rolled out the gate consisted of five or six trucks. First was the Husky Mounted Detection System (HMDS), usually driven by a smaller soldier because the cab was quite compact. The Husky was a one-seater with a Ground Penetrating Radar (GPR) panel system on the front; the GPR scanned for dense items buried underground as we drove a whopping five miles per hour at top speed.

This impressive system helps the operator determine if there is a Coke can buried three feet down or five-gallon jug two and a half feet down by scanning the ground's density as it rolls over. An experienced soldier can spot the less dense areas where an IED has been placed, surrounded by dense, packed ground that has not been disturbed.

Essentially, we were looking for loose pockets in dense dirt. If an operator missed an IED, it might be because the loose dirt on top had been blown away and the entire hole appeared to have the same density. The GPR system was a crucial piece of equipment we couldn't do our jobs without, and I was one of the soldiers trained on the details of this system.

The second truck in the convoy was the RG31, a category 1 Mine Resistant Ambush Protected (MRAP) vehicle. This is not a truck to be messed with.

Anyone crossing the street when this imposing behemoth was rolling their way was sure to pick up their step. The RG31 is made of armor plating, four-inch thick bulletproof glass, and metal cage fencing. Add in the insane rollers on the front and the massive tires taller than most civilian cars, and this would be the perfect vehicle to ride out the zombie apocalypse. It can roll over anything in its path and withstand a hit like you wouldn't believe.

The V-shaped chassis of the undercarriage is purposely designed to direct a blast up and out, pulling the chassis away from the rest of the truck, protecting the soldiers sitting inside. The heavy rollers in the front were specially designed to provide a massive amount of weight as we rolled along the ground.

In theory, the rollers in the front triggered the buried pressure plates and took the explosion, while the truck itself was unharmed. But it didn't take long for the terrorists to realize they needed to bury the pressure plates ten feet past the bomb: when the rollers set off the pressure plates, the truck would be sitting right on top of the bomb.

Next in the convoy was everyone's favorite truck, the Buffalo Mine Protected Clearance Vehicle. It was the big boy with six wheels, the Rolls Royce of all route clearance vehicles. This monstrous truck made the RG31 look like a civilian Hummer. Everyone wanted to be in this ride because you felt the safest in it; not even Osama Bin Laden himself could touch you. We lovingly referred to ours as the Bone Crusher. I got to ride in it quite often because it had the Common Remotely

Operated Weapons Station (CROWS), a weapon I was specially trained to use.

The CROWS is a remote weapon station mounted right in the truck, so we are able to engage the enemy with firepower without ever leaving the safety of the vehicle. I could see everything on the outside of the truck via a screen mounted on the inside.

For most missions, the CROWS was equipped with a .50-caliber machine gun, but sometimes we had a MK19 grenade launcher. I sat inside the truck to operate it, using the daylight camera, thermal camera and laser rangefinder. It worked a lot like a video game, and I used a specialized controller to direct the rifle 360 degrees and zoom in on my target.

Finally, bringing up the rear of the convoy were two more RG31s... a convoy can never have enough of those.

We were an imposing group of soldiers, cruising the terrain looking for IEDs. Though we looked like a mean bunch you wouldn't want to mess with, we knew we had to be smart.

We were out there every day sweeping for IEDs, and we needed the locals on our side. We weren't in a place to be making more enemies. The locals didn't choose this war and were at risk of being hurt or killed just as we were. As we rolled through each village, we would often hand out candy, bottles of water and toys to the kids who looked up at us in awe.

Their little faces would light up with pure joy as we tossed them soccer balls and M&M's. Until then it had always been the people back home that I was fighting for... my family, my country... but soon I realized that I was also fighting for these smiling faces, for their freedom as well as mine. We soon saw all our efforts at peace reciprocated.

The locals showed us where the IEDs were being buried, let us know who was traveling in the area, and kept us abreast of pertinent rumors they picked up on. With all of the help and intelligence we were gaining, it felt like we were teamed up with our own soldiers, those from different countries, and now the locals to stand together as one. The enemy was outnumbered in my book.

The days and the missions became routine: wake up at zero dark thirty (3:00 a.m.), gear up and roll out. We were well-oiled machines, uncovering IEDs left and right. Since we were consistently locating and removing bombs in the area, we were essentially rendering the work of the Taliban useless. They couldn't get a foothold with us on patrol. We were successfully protecting the area, and it felt mighty good. But spring was coming and with it the enemy forces were becoming more active. Things were about to take a turn for the worst.

Rolling out of the gates on one chilly morning, it seemed like any other typical day on the job. In actuality though, we were about to get our first real taste of war. I was driving the RG31 and we were jamming out to music in our headphones as we swept for IEDs. Suddenly a blast hit our truck. BOOM! We shot up in the air then smashed back down, hitting the ground hard.

Dust and powder were flying everywhere. The front tires were completely blown to bits. Everyone was quite shaken up, but we were all okay, and my wild side had just been rocked to life. It was like an insane roller coaster! I was grinning ear to ear as I turned to my truck commander riding shotgun, and shouted, "Let's do that again!" He looked at me like I had lost my mind and rightfully so. But as long as no one got hurt, I could do that all day!

I was soon snapped back to reality when one of our own was hurt. IEDs are no laughing matter. Each and every one could be life changing and life ending. I can't even begin to count the number of explosions I have been in, but there is certainly one that I will never forget. It was a beautiful, sunny day, but the roads were empty. The locals were all tucked away inside their homes or businesses. No one walked the street. No cars traveled past. It was an eerie feeling, knowing that something wasn't quite right, but not knowing where to look or what might be coming.

I was positioned in the turret, my hands wrapped around the .50-caliber rifle. I scanned the horizon, back and forth, back and forth. Movement out of the corner of my eye caught my attention. I turned to the right and saw a lone man standing in the woods, as if waiting for something. I trained my eyes on him, not looking away for one moment. Seconds later, the truck in front of us was hit from below by an IED and exploded into the air.

The blast was so powerful that I was whipped to the back of my turret and left with massive bruising on my side. As the dust and debris settled out of the air, we quickly assessed the gravity of the situation. The RG31 in front of us had flipped 180 degrees in the air and landed on its roof, facing my truck. I knew it was bad. I became enraged that we had been hit so hard and that my comrades were potentially injured or dead.

Profanities flew out of my mouth as I pinpointed the man in the woods, the one responsible for the bomb. He saw me locate him, fired a few shots at my truck and turned heel to run. I had him in my sights.

"LT, permission to fire?" I asked.

"No, Lane. I can't see anyone," my lieutenant responded.

"Sir, he is running away, and I have him in sight," I answered.

"No, Lane. If he isn't shooting at us, we can't fire back," my LT explained.

I was dumbfounded. I was watching the enemy sprint away. He would live another day. He would plant another bomb. He would take another life. I was furious.

I couldn't dwell on it now; my unit needed me. I regained my composure and turned to continue scanning for further enemy contact. I realized very quickly it was bad. The 800-pound IED that completely dismantled the truck immediately paralyzed Sergeant Daniel Rose from the chest down. In the blink of an eye, his entire life changed forever. As the medic worked to stabilize him, the rest of us locked down the area. Rose was quickly transported to the hospital and soon back to the States so he could receive the best possible care for his injuries.

After we managed to get the truck back to the base and get settled in the bunks, the events of the day really started to sink in. It was like a switch was flipped. Everything was different. One of our own was seriously hurt. He or any other member of our unit could have been killed. This was real. We were at war.

Life at the base continued on. We checked on Rose, getting reports about his status and recovery as he flew from Kandahar to Germany and back home. I am happy to report that he is doing well! We catch up every once in a while. He enjoys tackling a wide variety of paraplegic activities and is certainly living life to the fullest, but it was a long road to get him there.

But at FOB Wilson, we had to settle back into our routines.

* * *

A Little Breather

WE GOT A FEW DAYS OFF HERE AND THERE. ONE MIGHT WONDER what there is to do on a day off in the deserts of Afghanistan, but we managed to keep busy. There was a gym on the base, in case you weren't sweating enough by simply walking around in your uniform. Soldiers from other units would come to hang out and swap stories and vice versa. But the event that drew the most attention was a small boxing ring that the unit before us had built.

Using the skills I had gained while training in Jiu Jitsu in Mexico, I offered lessons to some of the guys in my unit, teaching them some of the basics of the mixed martial arts style of fighting. I bought some gloves and headgear, and I even built a wooden dummy for training. Soon we organized a regular fight night and some of the guys took turns sparring in matches. It was all in good fun and provided a needed respite from the rigors of the missions and the stress of the days.

We could let off a little steam, entertain the rest of the soldiers, and still walk away friends. It was quite a feeling knowing that we could all go at it in the ring, have a good time and take our wins and loses with grace.

On occasion I would head over to chat with the contractors the Army had hired to repair the trucks when the job was too specialized for us. It was always a treat to visit them because they had nicer things than we did, namely a grill. They regularly had burgers and barbecued ribs for dinner. Don't get me wrong, my pizzas were delicious, but nothing compared to sinking my teeth into a juicy, sizzling burger.

I had been completing missions for about six months when I finally got my first vacation. During a long deployment such as mine, each soldier gets two weeks of vacation and a round trip ticket to go anywhere they wanted. It was finally my turn. I decided to fly my wife to Acapulco, Mexico, somewhere I had never been, and spend part of my two weeks off with her there. I called my dad to let him know my plans in case he wanted to join Nadia and me.

"I'll be there," my dad said without hesitation. "I want to see you before you go back to Afghanistan."

He planned to stay the first week and fly home the second. I remember thinking it was a little crazy for my dad to fly all the way from Wisconsin just to see me for one week, but I was certainly glad that he did.

I was itching to get out of the sandbox and onto some Mexican beaches! Our hotel sat right on the shore, and we opened our windows at night to fall asleep to the crashing waves. We shopped at the little stands along the beach, dined at some amazing local joints and checked out all the tourist attractions. We even found an awesome mariachi band to play for us while we celebrated my return from Afghanistan with a little party. We relaxed on the warm sand with the waves gently pooling around our feet. It was a wonderful change from the burning sand and unbearable heat back in the Afghan desert.

After that first week, my dad had to head back home.

Anytime I recount this story, my eyes get misty and I get a little choked up. The conversation I had with my dad before he left is one that I will never forget as long as I live.

Standing outside the airport, his bag in his hand, my dad said, "Justin, I don't want you to go back. I have a bad feeling."

Something about the look in his eyes and the way he said it made me think it was more than a typical parent's worry.

The tough guy in me responded, "I will be good, Dad. Even if I lose my legs, I will be okay."

I hugged him and said, "Don't worry, Dad. I'll be fine. Really."

I actually *said* those words, *"Even if I lose my legs."* Looking back, it's still strikes me as an uncanny thing to say, given my situation now.

The U.S. Army had made me Army Strong and I could show that to my dad and try to alleviate his worry. But God had built me even stronger, I just didn't really know *how* strong.

4

BROTHER-IN-ARMS

Justin Ross
Date of Birth: September 14, 1988

L ife is full of good friends and memorable people; those that have your back, those that make you laugh, those whose company you enjoy, those incredibly smart ones that challenge you, and those fun ones you want to introduce to all your other friends. Justin Ross was all of those things.

Justin grew up in Howard, Wisconsin, in the Green Bay area, with a dad that was a pastor. Justin believed in two things: that Wisconsin would always have an abundance of snow in the winter... and that God is real.

Often, God's plan for our lives can seem a complete mystery; Justin was quite aware of this truth. He also knew that sometimes we need to be brought to our knees so we can grow in our Christian walk and draw closer to God. No one who is seemingly ordinary expects their life to be an extraordinary legacy to his friends and family, but that's exactly what Justin's life turned out to be.

What he left behind for his brothers-in-arms was a lesson in staying alive and fighting the good fight until you can't go on anymore.

Just like me, Ross decided to join the Army shortly after graduating high school. After his basic training and his AIT (the specific training for your chosen career path), he was placed with the brotherhood of the 428th Engineer Company, just as I was. This is where we met and began a friendship.

We shared the same first name and were both from Green Bay, so we loved to joke about our similarities and growing up in Wisconsin. We would toss names of friends and family back and forth, trying to find someone we both knew. After all Green Bay wasn't *that* big—we had to have a connection *somewhere* along the way!

We became friends because we had the same sense of humor and wit, and we shared the same out-of-the-box thinking that helped to bring growth and improvements to the 428. Our passions for being soldiers and the job itself were one and the same. The soldiers of the 428 were lucky to have him in the unit.

Every soldier out there loves a good PlayStation or Xbox game, and Justin was no exception. When we weren't out in the real world, we were playing pretend war in the tent. Being on different teams, we never patrolled together, so we played every chance we got (which wasn't as often as we would have liked). We did have online capabilities with the gaming consoles, but whenever the mood was solemn—like when our base was under fire or if a soldier was seriously injured—command would shut the internet down. They didn't want any family members learning of a loved one's death through social media. We were soon to experience just such a day.

Looking back, I wish I could have had more time to pick his brain for ideas and hear his funny anecdotes from back home. We were only a few short months into our deployment when Justin lost his life.

* * *

March 26, 2011

MARCH 26, 2011 WAS THE DAY THE TALIBAN TURNED MY HEART cold.

The First and Third Platoons were out on a mission to clear IEDs.

The day was beautiful and seemingly calm, until we experienced something none of us had ever faced before—a sniper. Ross was patrolling on foot, with two soldiers flanking either side. They had just placed metal rebar on both sides of the culvert. It was a mechanism our company specially designed to keep the enemy from placing IEDs inside each culvert.

Walking in a row, Ross and his team headed back toward the trucks. Somewhere, hiding among the trees or in a mud hut, a sniper saw his target. With three warm bodies to aim at, his best bet was firing at the center, increasing his chance for hitting a soldier. The sniper's bullet found Ross's helmet, piercing it completely through.

Justin dropped immediately and the two soldiers flanking him hit the ground, looking for cover. One glance at Ross and they knew he was gone.

One of them yelled, "Shots fired! Where is it coming from?" The next few minutes were that systematic controlled chaos that only soldiers can create and maintain. You often see it in war movies. Everyone took turns shouting their positions and what they did or did not see, guns trained at the tree line where the shot had rung out from. The gunners in the truck scanned every hiding place but couldn't spot the shooter. Ross's team moved with precision, keeping in tight formation to quickly drag his body onto one of the trucks.

Back at the base, the medics saw immediately there was nothing to be done for Ross. Word went up to command and the Internet was shut off.

That afternoon, with everyone back in the FOB, command ordered us to be in formation at 1700 hours, or 5:00 p.m. Normally, a formation at this time of day meant someone had earned a promotion or was getting an award, but that day every soldier on base knew neither of those reasons were why we were together. The air hung thick, pressing down on each of us. Scanning the crowd as each platoon got into formation, I could tell that even if they didn't know *what* specifically had happened, they knew why we were there. Fear, sadness and anger filled the eyes of every man on that base. Tears fell from the faces of those that knew Ross best.

Our commander, Captain Jim Servi, stood solemnly in front of us and took roll call to begin the ceremony. He called out the name and rank of a soldier.

"Here, sir!" the soldier shouted.

He called the name and rank of another soldier. "Here, sir!" came back the reply.

Then he called for Ross. "Specialist Justin Ross!"

There was silence.

"Specialist Justin Ross!"

This time the silence was filled with audible gasps and cries from the soldiers in the 428.

One last time, Captain Servi called, "Specialist Justin Ross!"

The silence was deafening. No one moved, breathed, or even blinked. We had lost a brother-in-arms.

Ross was gone.

We all stared through misty eyes at the display set up before us; the representation of a fallen soldier, the memory of Justin: His helmet balanced effortlessly atop his rifle, standing tall in the desert sand. His worn boots sat off to one side and his dog tags hung from the rifle, clinking in the warm breeze.

Our goal of going home as one unit was shattered. Our family had been broken. Each and every person in our unit would forever have something broken within them.

The ceremony ended, we broke formation, and most soldiers headed back to their tents with emotions high and their heads hung low. Some of us stayed behind on our knees in front of Ross's boots. We took a few moments to reflect on who he was at heart, our short friendships with him, and the legacy he would leave behind. One by one, our brothers stood, wiped their eyes, and headed back, attempting to fill their minds with other thoughts while still trying to honor Ross's memory.

I was the last soldier to leave.

* * *

R.I.P. Justin Ross

Ross's tragic death hit me harder than I expected. I grew quiet and solemn. My jokester personality was gone. My platoon leader picked up on how devastating the loss was for me and told me to take a day or two off to gather myself.

More than anything I wanted to immediately get back out there and start hunting, but I knew he was right. I knew this because the only focus in my mind was taking out each and every Taliban fighter holding a gun, whether their back was to me or not. I needed to calm down and refocus, but I was furious. That moment had been the last straw for me.

After a week or so, my personality returned to somewhat normal, but slightly under the surface was an anger that was boiling. It would rise to the surface and change who I was while out on a mission. Through my scope, I was searching deep into the hills, scanning the roads with more intensity.

I was waiting for my moment—I was hunting my prey. I wanted to avenge the death of my friend.

The days seemed to slow. The missions felt more intense. My thoughts turned a little darker. I was more commanding and stronger. I no longer dreamed of going home to my wife and family. I did everything I could to ensure a prolonged stay in Afghanistan to continue fighting. The furthest thought from my mind was going home. There was nothing but the war. There was only the enemy and myself...taking them out one-by-one...until they took me out.

There is a verse in Proverbs that advises one to guard their heart, because everything you do will flow from there. I saw that clearly as hatred gripped my heart. My thoughts were consumed with revenge; it has the power to change who you are at the core. Slowly, I was turning away from the man God desired me to be as I rejected thoughts of forgiveness and compassion. It's easy to forget that God is in charge, that he has a perfect plan, and we are all under his watch and care.

Things happen for a reason, even if that reason isn't clear to us. Even when we veer off course, God has this way of disrupting *our* carefully laid plans and molding them back into his own. Clearly, my anger, my hate and my plan of self-destruction didn't fit into the plans he had for me. He was going to use me how he saw fit: for the future he had already planned for me. I was his tool, not my own, nor the Army's, but his alone.

But how could God take this broken man, so full of hate, pain and selfishness, and use him for a higher purpose?

5

WHAT A BLAST!

Two months after Ross's death, I celebrated my twenty-third birthday. It wasn't the biggest and best birthday celebration I've had by any means, but I was alive and that was all I could really ask for while working and fighting in a war zone. As it turns out, it was the last "normal" birthday I would ever have.

I've said it several times now, but I'll say it again: everything that happens in this world, good or bad, is directed by God. At this point in my story, you may be wondering how I could still believe that after seeing one brother-in-arms paralyzed and one shot to death, but deep down I still wholeheartedly believed it. The details of what happened next are how I know that God has been with me from the start—watching over my life and directing my own personal story.

I will start with one little ironic detail: July 2, 2011, was my day off. I repeat: This was my DAY OFF.

My platoon sergeant came charging into the tent at zero dark thirty and woke everyone up. He had just realized he needed a few more troops for the day's mission. He asked if anyone wanted to volunteer, and I thought since I didn't have anything better to do, I'd go.

I got dressed and gathered my gear, weapons and snacks. The sudden change of plans got me cranked up and excited to get out there.

Who knew what the day might hold!? I hopped in the RG31 and climbed in the turret to sit behind the .50-caliber rifle. As we drove through the final gate of the FOB, I glanced back, not knowing this would be the last time I ever saw my home base... the tents, the chow hall, the boxing ring...

The day's mission required us to clear the most dangerous route in our area of operation (AO). We would clear it not once, but twice. It would be the second time that brought so much devastation.

We were on the way to Red Stripe, our first route of the day. Red Stripe had flat farmland on one side of the road and a large mud wall with mud huts standing just beyond it on the other side. Our convoy had cleared this dirt road a hundred times before. We'd rolled over quite a few IEDs in the trucks before as well but suffered no real injuries from the blasts. This was just another day on the job.

Within the first ten minutes on the road—BOOM! The RG31 in front of mine was hit by a one-hundred-pound IED. The massive armored vehicle smashed down for a hard landing, leaving it inoperable. The wheels were completely blown off the truck, and while the engine wasn't gone entirely, it suffered severe damage.

Fortunately, no one in the truck was touched by the blast, and were all able to exit the truck on their own. They were shaken up, of course... you never really got used to being "blown up," but they were still breathing and that's all you can ask for after an IED finds you. The soldiers were checked out by the medic while the platoon leader called back to base to have the Quick Reaction Force (QRF) come out. The QRF was a rapid response unit trained to offer assistance in developing situations. They brought us a replacement truck and a fresh crew, along with a new medic since ours was among the soldiers in the blast.

Before we headed out again, my driver asked if he could get behind the gun for the rest of the mission. He was trying to earn an award for so many hours spent behind the gun. I had already earned mine and didn't mind driving, so we switched. I climbed behind the wheel and we continued clearing our routes.

Later in the day, we headed back out on Red Stripe to clear it for the second and final time. We were expecting an easy go of it since we had already cleared it once, but this time we were slightly on edge. No one was watching from the fields as they usually did as we rolled by. Odd. We were getting close to the crater where the first truck had taken a hit earlier. Food was on all of our minds. We were starving and lunch was still a few hours away.

"I'm gonna have a big, juicy, medium-rare steak and baked potato with all the trimmings, and an entire plate of hot, fresh rolls," I said.

"Yea? Keep dreaming!" Staff Sergeant Daniel Kienow laughed.

"What about one of those famous Lane pizza pies?" Specialist Aaron Krueger volunteered.

Suddenly, something grabbed Kienow's attention. He peered into the tree line. "Keep an eye out, Krueger," his said in a commanding voice. "Movement in the bushes."

We all turned to get a look. Someone called out, "Suspicious male. Nine o'clock."

Seconds later, a 200-pound IED exploded beneath our truck. Earth engulfed us. The truck was thrown into the air and then slammed back down on its right passenger side. The blast tore through our truck and ripped off the driver side door. I was crammed inside, my adrenaline pumping, not knowing the extent of my injuries, and my Army training took over.

I yelled for my battle buddies, "Krueger! Check in!" My gunner did not respond. "Specialist Krueger!" I craned my neck to try and get a look at him. He was stunned and working to get himself straightened out. Once he regained his bearings, he crawled over and popped his head through the space between the sideways driver and passenger seats.

"You guys okay?" he asked. I checked my pants and found them covered in blood. It was easy to see my right arm was snapped in half. I reported back to Krueger. From beneath me came a plea from Kienow in the passenger seat. "Get off me, Lane! I can't breathe!"

I had landed on top of him after the blast and crushed the air from his lungs with the full weight of my body. I used my good left arm to pull myself up while pushing off of him with my broken right arm. This would have been an excruciating movement had adrenaline not been coursing through my veins.

I looked down at my pants again. The blood oozed from my legs and covered everything in the truck. I didn't know how bad it was, but I knew that there couldn't be that much blood without a massive injury.

I started repeating, "I'm messed up. I'm messed up." I heard shouting outside the truck, my unit scrambling to get to us. Specialist Jay Kroeplin reached into the truck to pull me out. And everything went black.

* * *

NOT ONLY WAS GOD WATCHING OVER AND PROTECTING ME, HE WAS placing the right people in the right place at the right time to help me. He knew just who to put in my path to give me the best possible outcome.

Many people want to blame devastating, traumatic events on God. We never seem to realize that the bad things that happen come from people or events surrounding us in the world. The *strength* that we use to overcome these bad things—*that* is what comes from God.

Here is the story from my fateful day, retold by those that had been placed in my path by God.

* * *

Specialist Jared Warren's Account

TECHNICALLY, I WASN'T EVEN SUPPOSED TO BE ON MISSION that day.

I was the medic assigned to Third Platoon, and July 2nd was supposed to be our rest and refit day. That meant our primary tasks for the day were to do maintenance on the trucks, weapons and other equipment, as well as personal tasks like laundry. It also meant that we were QRF for the company while First and Second Platoons were on mission.

It was late morning when I heard that First Platoon had been hit along Route Red Stripe. As QRF, it was our job to escort our team of mechanics to the blast site with their flatbed and crane trucks to pick up the damaged vehicle and get it back to base. When we got to the blast site, we also moved the soldiers from the damaged vehicle into our convoy for transport back to the base hospital. The medic who had originally ridden out with First Platoon that day decided to ride back with the soldiers that had been involved in the blast to ensure some consistency in their care throughout the process.

This meant First Platoon was now without a medic. They were also down by a gun truck, and that had been damaged in the blast. To solve both of those issues, the gun truck that I was riding in was assigned to finish the day with First Platoon. I was their new medic. We fell in line and were the second truck from the rear of the convoy.

We finished clearing Red Stripe beyond the blast site and moved on to clear the rest of the routes that First Platoon had been assigned that day. The last assignment was to clear Red Stripe a second time, which we started in mid-afternoon.

Moving west to east along the route, we cleared the first half without incident. After passing FOB Kandalay, we entered a pomegranate orchard. We had just gotten to the vicinity of the morning's blast site when a second bomb went off. It was behind my truck, and I could tell from the sound of the blast that it had been a big one.

At our location in Afghanistan, everything was covered in a very fine dirt that everyone called moon dust. When a bomb went off, that moon dust was thrown into the air and created a dirty cloud so thick that there were times I couldn't even see the end of my rifle. Now, as I turned inside my truck to try to see where the blast had been and if any of our trucks had gotten hit, all I could see was dust. I had completely lost visibility of the rear gun truck.

Right away, the radios started chattering with everyone trying to figure out what was happening. I remember someone in the Buffalo saying that the rear gun truck had been hit and forcibly tossed entirely off the roadway.

The truck I was in had a gyro-cam which I lifted up and spun around to try to see above the dust cloud. When the dust finally began to clear, I could see the rear gun truck lying on the passenger side, off the route, and no one seemed to be moving from inside.

As I prepared my gear to get ready to jump out of the truck, the Buffalo began turning around to check the blast crater for any secondary

IEDs. Turning a Buffalo around on that narrow route was no small feat, but the driver was skillfully able to execute his multi-point turn. The truck was now facing back to the west, the direction from where we had just come.

In order to safely move from wherever my position in a convoy might be to another vehicle that had been damaged by a bomb, I would often use the other vehicles in the convoy line as stepping-stones. By climbing up and over one vehicle and onto the next, I was able to minimize the time that my feet were on the ground, therefore making it less likely that I would step on any secondary IEDs.

I utilized this method now, leaving my truck via the rear door and moving to the back ladder of the Buffalo directly in front of me. As I opened the door of my truck and stepped out, I distinctly remember thinking that the pomegranate field along the north side of the road would make an excellent hiding spot for an ambush. A very clear thought went through my head that this was probably going to be the day that I got shot.

With that in mind, I swiveled my rifle to the north to scan for threats as I moved to the Buffalo. However, just as I stepped out and brought my rifle up, an Apache gunship dropped in above the orchard and started making very low passes across the tops of the trees.

Clearly, that pilot had also decided that the orchard represented the biggest threat to our convoy and was going to make sure no one popped their head up from that side to bother us. With the north side covered, I spun to cover the south while I ran the remaining distance to the truck.

I climbed up inside the Buffalo and waited as they drove back to the blast crater, using the arm to drag through the dirt and debris to ensure that there were no remaining pieces of the bomb or secondary bombs that could go off. Once they said it was clear, I climbed back down and ran to the damaged vehicle.

It was laying on its passenger side about ten feet off the road. The engine and front axle were mostly gone, scattered about the area when they were ripped off from the main body of the truck, just as they were designed to do when a bomb hit. I ran along the bottom of the truck, which was now the side closest to the road, until I got to the back door of the truck. I tried but couldn't get it open, so I continued around the back end of the truck to the top, which was the side facing away from the road into the field.

These particular trucks had two hatches in the roof, one of which I was able to quickly get open and poke my head inside to assess what was going on.

The gunner was sitting inside, obviously a little bit dazed, but did not appear to be bleeding at all. He looked up when I stuck my head in, and I asked him if he was hurt anywhere. He was very calm, and said that he didn't think so, but that the guys up in the front of the truck needed help right away. I told him to sit tight and wait until I came back for him, and then I quickly ran to the front of the truck, where I was finally able to climb up on top.

The driver's door was basically gone. There were a few twisted pieces of metal still hanging on in a couple places, but it opened, and I had direct access to Lane in the driver's seat. He was partially conscious, although I could see that something had smashed him in the face because he was bleeding from the nose and mouth. He was hanging from his seat belt, dangling into the passenger side below him. He wasn't moving very much.

From below Lane, I could hear his Truck Commander (TC), Staff Sergeant Kienow, yelling that he felt like he was being crushed and was having a hard time breathing.

I started talking to Lane, and even though he would move around a little bit, he couldn't respond much more than moaning or grunting. I told him that I needed him to pull the ripcord that would allow his body armor to come apart because I couldn't reach it. He managed to get it pulled about halfway, and then lost the strength to pull it any further.

By this time, a few more guys had made it to the truck and a lot of things happened very quickly all at once. Specialist Kroeplin—we called him Corky—climbed up on the top side of the truck with me, and we started the process of lifting Lane out. At the same time, I yelled down to Sergeant Dustin Bowden, who was on the ground because he had a radio and could relay the information to Second Lieutenant Micha Swanson to call in a medical evacuation (MEDEVAC) request. He also told some of the other truck drivers to send somebody down with the backboards that were attached to every vehicle.

I looked toward the front of the convoy and saw a soldier running with one of the requested backboards. Most of the medics in the company had taped extra equipment to the boards that might be useful if the board was ever needed. Clear as day, I saw whoever was running at me rip all of that stuff off the board and frisbee it out of the way into the field as he ran.

I was, simultaneously, talking to Staff Sergeant Kienow down below us, still in the truck, trying to get an idea of his injuries and how bad of shape he was in.

Corky and I managed to hook our arms under both of Lane's arms and started to lift him out. Because there was so little room on top of the truck to maneuver, and because we still hadn't been able to get his armor off, we were only able to get him about halfway out before we ran out of leverage and room to work.

I carried a strap with me on every mission that was specifically designed for moving patients in a variety of ways. I pulled it out and got it threaded under Lane's arms, which gave us just enough extra leverage to pull him the rest of the way out of the truck. As his hips cleared the door frame, before we could even lay him on a backboard, someone shouted, "Doc, do you want tourniquets down here?"

I looked down at Lane and for the first time was able to see the extent of the damage. Both of his legs were mangled from about mid-thigh down, and I couldn't see anything that I recognized as a foot.

"Yes!" I shouted. "I need tourniquets on both sides!"

God bless the combat lifesaver training that everyone had gone through prior to deployment. No sooner than I had said he needed tourniquets, two or three guys from the ground climbed to the top of the truck with a handful of tourniquets between them. They descended on Lane and wrapped his legs to shut the bleeding off.

Once the tourniquets were in place, I really wanted to get off the top of the truck. We were sitting ducks up there and I was still worried about an ambush coming from the pomegranate orchard to the north. We picked up Lane on the backboard and handed him down to the guys on the ground, using the tipped over vehicle as cover from the north. While the other guys went back to get Staff Sergeant Kienow out, I jumped down to attend further to Lane.

I made sure Lane had a clear airway and was still breathing. Then I rechecked his tourniquets to make sure they were still tight after moving him around. I started an IV to run some fluids in an attempt to keep his blood pressure up. (To any medical personnel out there: I know, I know —it was 2011 and volume expanders were still protocol.)

Staff Sergeant Kienow was extracted from the truck and they laid him down beside Lane. I could see he had a nasty open lower leg fracture, but it wasn't bleeding profusely and was not a direct life threat. When I asked him what else hurt, he said he was fine except for his leg. I told him to just hang out and keep calm, and I would get to his leg just as quickly as I could.

The gunner, Kreuger, made it out of the vehicle and sat on the ground beside the truck, and he was *pissed*. Actually, "pissed" doesn't even begin to describe his level of anger. "Irate" might get you halfway there. He was cursing and screaming at the Taliban something fierce, demanding we find his weapon so that he could show them how he felt. He was also on about a two-minute loop. He would repeat the questions he had asked and everything he said roughly every couple of minutes. This is a classic symptom of a concussion/traumatic brain injury. Unfortunately, there wasn't a whole lot I could do for that in the field, so I assigned one guy to sit with him and keep him where he was, and *definitely* not give him a weapon.

A patrol from the nearby infantry FOB showed up with a couple of trucks and a bunch of guys. I still don't know if it was a scheduled patrol or a QRF, but they were poking up the route as if nothing had happened. When I saw them coming, I yelled for them to get over here and help out, and they hopped right to it. Thankfully they had a medic with them, and I sent him to look at Staff Sergeant Kienow's leg. When I checked on them later, the infantry medic was already splinting and dressing the injury.

The first sergeant with them informed me that the MEDEVAC bird was on the way, and that they were going to use the landing zone at the FOB to load everyone up. We would use their trucks to transport the patient back to the base and wait for the bird.

I soon heard a helicopter overhead. When I looked up, I saw the MEDEVAC bird with the flight medic hanging out the side door pointing towards us, or at least at the relative blast area. My thought at the time was "Yep, big boom here!"

Knowing that MEDEVAC was so close and headed towards the FOB, we loaded Lane and Kreuger in the infantry's first truck and sent them on their way. I went back to get Staff Sergeant Kienow, and, as we were carrying him to the next truck, a guy with a flight helmet popped around the corner and asked what we had. It was odd seeing him, because I knew we were too far away from the FOB for any of the MEDEVAC crew to come visit us. I asked what he was doing there, and he said they had just landed the bird on the route behind the convoy. We thought they had been headed to the FOB!

We pulled Staff Sergeant Kienow back out of the truck and carried him over to the helicopter while I gave the flight medic a run down on all three guys and the specific medical attention we had given each one. The bird was about one hundred yards down the route in a nice, big clearing. We loaded Staff Sergeant Kienow and moved off to the side. They waited for the truck with Lane and Kreuger to get turned around at the FOB and come back to transfer them over. I should have stuck around to help with that transfer, but I had a lot of stuff to sort out back at the blast site, so I headed back that way. About two minutes later, I heard the bird carrying Lane pick up and go screaming off towards Kandahar. Minutes later, Kienow and Kreuger took off in another bird.

Third Platoon came back out with QRF, and it took us a long time to clean everything up and clear the site. It was dark when we finally hit the fuel point at FOB Pasab (also known as FOB Wilson) to fill the trucks. I jumped out and ran over to find the patrol leader to see if he had any news on Lane, Kienow, or Kreuger. He did not.

When we got back to the motor pool, the company commander and first sergeant were impatiently awaiting our arrival and made a beeline straight for me, which is never a good sign. I held my breath, expecting the worst. I was unbelievably relieved when they told me Lane was still in surgery, but alive.

When the company left Afghanistan, we went through a demobilization process at Fort Dix, New Jersey. Lane was still at Walter Reed Army Medical Center (WRAMC) while we were at Fort Dix, and I tried everything I could to organize a trip to see him, considering it was only about an hour drive. It took days to get the request to leave the base processed. I don't know what level had to approve it, but apparently it went pretty high up the chain.

I rented a van and was preparing to drive six or seven of us over to see him. The day before the trip, I found out that he was being transferred out of WRAMC. I never did get to see him while the unit was at Fort Dix.

To this day, I still think that not being able to visit him due to the bureaucratic process of getting the trip approved was about the dumbest thing ever.

* * *

Staff Sergeant Daniel Kienow's Account

THE MORNING OF JULY 2, 2011 STARTED LIKE ANY OTHER MORNING that the platoon went out on mission. First Platoon had the early route clearing mission that day. In the pre-dawn hours, all the soldiers went to the motor pool to prep the vehicles, test the radios and mount the weapons systems. I was the assistant patrol leader and, I think, the patrol leader for this particular mission was Second Lieutenant Swanson. The two of us went to the company TOC (Tactical Operations Center) to get the most current intelligence information for the routes we would be clearing that day.

Around 0530 the platoon gathered together to receive the mission brief, and then we had about a ten-minute window to run to the chow hall for a quick breakfast. All the vehicles were running and ready to go for a 0600 SP (Start of Patrol). As the platoon headed out, I radioed the TOC and gave them the number of vehicles, personnel and weapons going out on mission. Because I was the assistant patrol leader, my vehicle, an RG31, was in the rear and responsible for rear security.

What was unusual about that day was the fact that we would be clearing Route Red Stripe *twice*. Normally, it was cleared once a day by one of the two route clearing patrols that were sent out. Historically, Red Stripe was a hot spot for enemy contact in one form or another. Roughly one month earlier, my truck and the same crew plus a medic, Specialist

(Doc) Eric Wright, had been blown up on this route. Fortunately, we all walked away, but the RG31 received significant damage. As a result, we had an older RG31 that I believe had been refurbished from previous IED explosions.

Route Red Stripe was one of the first routes to be cleared that morning. From our base, FOB Wilson (later known as FOB Pasab), we headed east down Highway 1, entered Red Stripe from the east end and the traveled west. The route was a dirt road that ran parallel to the black top highway. To my knowledge, there had never been an IED strike on the east end of Red Stripe since we had been in the country. The west half was the complete opposite and had seen quite a few IEDs planted.

We moved at a snail's pace of five to ten miles an hour as we cleared the road from the east to the west. At approximately 0900 there was an IED strike to one of the vehicles in the patrol. Dirt and debris flooded the air. Staff Sergeant Ryan Ratliff's truck had taken the brunt of the blast. I had communications with the battlespace owner, the Stryker Cavalry Regiment based in FOB Kandalay, and informed them of what was going on. Second Lieutenant Swanson coordinated with our company for a QRF.

While the two of us were on the radio, other trucks were conducting sweeps of the area looking for secondary IED's. Once the area was deemed safe, the occupants in the damaged truck were evacuated. The vehicle had to be towed, but thankfully all occupants were able to walk away on their own. One of the soldiers on board the truck that got hit was the platoon medic Doc Wright.

He needed to be evacuated with the rest of the troops, so the QRF medic, Specialist Jared Warren, joined our convoy to replace him. Doc Wright didn't appear to be hurt, but it was standard practice that anyone involved in an IED blast had to get evaluated no matter what. It took roughly two hours from the time of the IED strike until we were ready to continue the mission.

We finished clearing Route Red Stripe, exited onto Highway 1 and proceeded west toward FOB Pasab/FOB Wilson. The second route to be cleared that day was Route Summit. It ran directly south of Pasab and was also a dirt road along a black top road. It was usually an uneventful route. The third route was a dirt road that jogged west off of Route Summit and had a history of IEDs.

Our platoon had suffered at least one prior IED strike. The Husky driver had been blown up while investigating a suspected IED. The driver was okay, and the vehicle sustained little damage.

It was around noon when we started the third route. The platoon spent several hours sweeping it, not because it was a particularly long route, but because in the ditch on both sides there grew a tall variety of reed grass. It was an excellent hiding place for the enemy to crouch down in and for placing IEDs. On several occasions, we had attempted to burn all the vegetation out of the ditch, and we tried again unsuccessfully this day. The grass appeared to be dry but there was enough moisture on the ground that any fire we lit quickly died out. It was close to 1400 hours by the time the platoon rolled back on to Highway 1 and then on to Red Stripe for the second time. This time we would enter from the west side and clear to the east.

We were approximately a third of the way into the route when the gun truck ahead of us spotted suspicious activity. Through thermal sites, the gunner saw two men running parallel to our convoy. Sergeant Nathan McCartney, the gun truck commander, relayed via radio what the gunner had seen. I asked Krueger, who was behind a .50-caliber machine gun, if he had eyes on any persons running. He said he did. Because of the rules of engagement and because we were not able to report them as a credible threat with hostile intent, all I could do for the moment was to tell him to keep his gun trained on them. They had no visible weapons and none of the vehicles ahead of us had spotted any possible IEDs. At that moment, our truck was directly over the same spot as the IED strike that had hit our patrol earlier that morning.

Red Stripe was a washboard, pothole-filled dirt road. The area we were occupying was particularly bad, filled with deep potholes full of water that made travel difficult. Trying to avoid the holes made it somewhat predictable to the enemy where our vehicles would have to drive. There was a rather large water-filled mud hole on the driver's side. To my knowledge, Lane did not drive through the hole, but what happened in the brief moment after talking to Krueger, I can't remember. Once second it was quiet, and the next I heard a blast and saw a flash of dirt and mud splatter over the windshield.

I am not sure how long I was unconscious, maybe a couple of minutes, but it could have been as much as five or ten. When I came to, I realized right away that the truck was lying on the passenger side. I couldn't see anything out of the windshield, but I could hear vehicles outside, most likely sweeping for secondary IEDs before dismounting any soldiers. I had a deep cut on the inside of my mouth and spit out a rough piece of glass. I tried to move, but I was pinned underneath the wreckage. I had a strap cutter on my body armor specifically for cutting seat belts, a tool I thought I would never have to use. I was able to cut off my seatbelt but that didn't help; I still couldn't move. I didn't feel any pain, but I could tell that something was not right with my left leg. I mentally crossed my fingers and hoped that maybe it was just a bad sprain. Surprisingly—at six foot two and 180 pounds—I didn't get claustrophobic cramped up in that small wrecked space. In my mind I focused on remaining as calm as possible. I knew help was coming as fast as it safely could. Given my pinned-down situation, I couldn't physically do anything to help. The only thing I could do was reassure and comfort Lane and Krueger.

Within a minute or so of regaining consciousness, I tried to check in with them both. Lane answered, but there was no response from Krueger. As I talked with Lane, I could feel a warm liquid dripping on my face. My first thought was that it was oil leaking from the engine, but had I rationally thought about it, oil wouldn't have made any sense. It would have been scalding hot and the engine was in front of me, not on top of me. Had I realized that what I felt was a significant amount of Lane's blood, panic would have set in. As it was, I couldn't even turn my head to look up at him, so I couldn't see the blood; I could only feel it.

We asked each other if the other was okay. I don't recall his initial response, but he sounded fairly calm. I don't think that reality of the situation had set in. I told him that I was pinned down and couldn't move, that I thought he was on top of me. I asked if he was able to move so that I might be able to get out.

That's when he replied, "I'm really messed up."

I was unable to see him, so the best and the only thing I could do was to keep talking to him. I told Lane that he would be okay and that the others in the platoon were coming to get us out. About that time, Krueger regained consciousness and Lane's voice slowly faded out.

Krueger asked if I was okay and I said "Yes." He then said he couldn't find his weapon. I told him not to worry about it, but it seemed to be bothering him. His voice changed to an angry tone; he said he hated Afghanistan and the Taliban. Then he asked me again if I was okay and again told me he couldn't find his weapon. Krueger once more explicitly expressed his hatred for the Taliban. This cycle when on for some time.

At some point, the other soldiers finished conducting the secondary sweeps around our vehicle and started to pull Lane out. I don't remember what was said and how long it took to remove him, but the next soldier I saw was Specialist Kroeplin. I could finally move, and I told him I could pull myself out.

I crawled out and sat on the overturned vehicle. It felt good to be out of that small space. Kroeplin asked how I was. I told him I was okay, but something was wrong with my left ankle. He helped me to the ground, and we hobbled over to a medic, who was with an infantry platoon that was operating in the same area. By that time, I think Lane had already been evacuated via helicopter to Kandahar Airfield (KAF).

I lay down and the young medic, a private, carefully cut off my left boot to expose my ankle. He then pulled off my sock, and that was when the pain hit me. I cursed him out for cutting off my boot but not cutting off my socks and immediately felt bad about it; he was just trying to help. Shortly after that, a chopper arrived and flew Krueger and me to the field hospital at KAF. We held hands the entire way.

When we arrived, they put me on a gurney and escorted me to the ER. They took my blood-stained uniform and cleaned me up as best they could. I was taken to an open bay with other soldiers with similar type injuries. I didn't know where Lane and Krueger had been taken.

That evening the brigade commander, a Navy captain, gave me a Purple Heart medal and a phone to call my wife. She had already been told the news, but the details had been distorted. She was told I had been injured by an IED while dismounted, so she was relieved to hear my voice and my real story.

Sometime around midnight I was taken to the operating room. I had a lower tibia and fibula fracture. I was fitted with an external fixation device, which looked like a cage around my left foot, that was held in place by screws into my shin and ankle.

The next morning Krueger came to visit me. I asked if he knew anything about Lane. He said it was not good but didn't know any details. About two hours later, I was flown to a hospital in Germany. That was where I finally got to see Lane. He was on the intensive care floor in a coma and he did not look good. But as you know by now... looks are often deceiving.

* * *

Captain Jim Servi's Account

THERE ARE DAYS IN YOUR LIFE THAT YOU LOOK BACK ON AND KNOW that you will never forget them: graduation, the freedom of leaving home, getting married, the birth of a child. Those happy memories stay with you forever.

Sometimes, unfortunately, so do the negative ones: tragedy, losing a loved one, or watching the soldiers you love get blown up by a terrorist's IED. Afghanistan left me with many of those tragic memories, but also with many happy memories that I will never forget. Watching Justin rise from near death at the hands of evil to become an inspiration to everyone he meets has been a truly joyful experience.

That blistering, hot day in July is one that I'll never forget; yet, much of it is a blur. This odd contradiction is something that often leaves me in confusion. Specific details are hard to recall, but the physical and emotional pain we all experienced that day comes flooding back instantly upon recollection.

Activity among hostiles never stopped, but it had slowed over the winter and then started picking up again in March. The battlespace (our area of operation) owner that we were working with along Red Stripe was conducting a CONOP (concept of operation) to target IED emplacers. Hearing this news alleviated some of the uneasiness I had about travel along that route. Knowing that a team was out there eliminating IEDs along one of our most active roadways would make our jobs easier.

When I was approached to ask if we could clear the route *twice* that day, I didn't hesitate. My team had done it several times before and it was an effective way to support the CONOP. Plus, in the back of my head I thought, "With a team out there targeting IED emplacers, it should be a quiet day on the route." I was wrong.

First Platoon was assigned the route for both iterations that day and, I believe, Third Platoon was on QRF.

Linebacker hit an IED on Red Stripe.

The message had come over the Blue Force Tracker, the system we use to track friendly and hostile military forces, and we began monitoring on multiple communication devices with our battle space owners.

My heart always sank hearing those messages, and the anxiety of the unknown ramped me up to fight. Sometimes a message like that meant only a small IED, no damage, and the patrol kept on moving; at other times, it was life-threatening. Not knowing what the assessment was those first few minutes after an IED attack, our TOC (Tactical Operation Center) was wired and impatiently waiting for more information. When a patrol hit an IED, they must coordinate with their battlespace first, then MEDEVAC if necessary, and our company headquarters last. Helplessly waiting was unbearable.

We were soon able to breathe sighs of relief as the message came directly to the company headquarters.

No injuries, CASEVAC requested for precaution. Will swap vehicle with QRF.

The QRF had been anxiously waiting as well with a vehicle from Third Platoon. Doc Warren took over as the combat medic for the patrol.

As soon as the vehicle returned with the soldiers, I went over to speak with them as I always try to do after a SIGACT (significant activity). Naturally, they were shaken up, but everyone appeared to be fine. Doc Wright confirmed no injuries, and they headed back to their tents for a shower and some much-needed rest.

The patrol out on IED duty continued. After completing several other routes without incident, they headed back to Red Stripe. It was scheduled to be the last route of the day.

After passing a patrol base, they entered a dangerous area where there had been several other IED incidents. Specialist Justin Lane was driving, Staff Sergeant Dan Kienow was the TC and Specialist Aaron Krueger was the gunner for the lead vehicle. All of a sudden, hell was unleashed. A 200-pound IED, made from highly explosive material, ripped through vehicle and did something that no other IED had ever done: it penetrated the vehicle. It tore into the truck near the left corner where Justin's leg had been applying pressure to the gas pedal and turned the cab into a mangled mess of metal.

A short time later, while monitoring the battlespace communications, the company TOC was informed of the IED blast. Seconds seemed like hours as we helplessly waited for more information. Each report we received was worse than the last, from both the Battle Space net and the messages we had begun to receive through company communication systems. MEDEVAC was enroute and we received a report that it was life threatening.

"Oh my God, this can't be happening," was all I could think. I wished I could do something. I had no idea what was actually happening on the ground, and we tried to piece it together over the hours and days after the event. After the MEDEVAC departed, which came from our battalion medical team, all I could do was wait for more information. Our team was closely monitoring the situation and movements of the area. The injuries were extensive, more than I had ever heard from one accident, and the prognosis was critical. We tracked Justin's movement: Landstuhl Regional Medical Center in Germany was the next stop. For days following the IED blast, no one was sure whether he would live. One of the toughest parts of this whole situation was that I would not get to see him for months; instead I relied on updates from others, and we were still deep in the fight.

I felt helpless. I didn't sleep for days. I was up at night, wondering what would happen to Justin, but I knew that I had to refocus and try to prevent this from happening to anyone else.

When the patrol returned that evening, First Sergeant Derek Andrasic and I met everyone at the motor pool. We gave them the only updates that we had. Some wanted to talk, and we listened. Others simply wanted to go back to their bunks and digest what had just happened. Some needed hugs as tears streamed down their cheeks. Everyone had to process it in their own way.

For me, I remained in the motor pool long after everyone left. Solitude and reflection are where I always find answers and peace. Alone, I prayed, and God was listening. He took care of Justin.

* * *

Captain SK Alfstad's Account

BEING WITH YOUR JOES IN "THE SUCK" WAS IMPORTANT FOR chaplains. However, I was not looking forward to getting my brain rattled, or worse, in an IED blast. Even so, I think I gained a lot of respect from Third Platoon on one of our first missions together.

I started out in a sideways seat in the back of the RG31. We went by a few mud brick villages. They all looked the same. There was absolutely nothing distinct about them: mud brick building after mud brick building, all a single story. The villages had makeshift graveyards on the outskirts. The peasant's graves were marked with rocks. The more esteemed, or well-to-do, had a flag marking their internment. And of course, there was dust, dust and more dust.

I was constantly concerned about the toll it might be taking on our lungs. To say the roads were rough would be an understatement. After about an hour and a half into the journey on my sideways seat, I was extremely queasy. The truck commander spoke to me through the headsets we all wore.

"How are you doing, sir?" he asked.

I wanted to suck it up and be tough, but I admitted, "I think I'm going to have to use this empty Doritos bag to hurl in."

I was ever more thankful for the availability of that piece of trash.

The always cool and considerate Second Lieutenant Swanson gestured to the driver. I don't know what his non-verbal movement meant, but I could tell the driver understood. A minute or two later, we stopped for a stretch break. It was a remote spot that the lieutenant was confident wasn't laden with IEDs. By now, he had a pretty good understanding of the Taliban's TTP (tactics, terrain, and personnel) in that area.

After a bathroom, smoke, and stretch break, it was time to mount up again. The lieutenant said to me, "Sir, why don't you sit up front? The ride is better."

I kind of felt like a wuss taking him up on his offer, but the nausea I felt from the motion sickness was miserable. It dawned on me that nausea was just one of the factors these Route Clearance Patrol (RCP) soldiers dealt with. These were tough young men. I've heard infantry, and even Special Forces, say they wouldn't want to do the RCP mission. But this is what JP did, and 3-1 was his platoon.

JP and I formed a strong bond. We were on this mission together and seemed to have an instant rapport. He came to me for advice and insight on a few occasions. As it turned out, we had the same interest and passion for helping underprivileged kids. He wanted to be a part of my non-profit outreach program back home. I knew he would be a great asset.

I felt like we were kindred spirits; he was my protégé in a sense. We both had some free time to discuss the vision for us working together, and shortly after he went out on another routine mission. However, this one was anything but "routine."

His vehicle was struck by an IED. He lost both legs, broke his arm, sustained multiple serious internal injuries and suffered a TBI (traumatic brain injury). He was at Walter Reed Army Medical Center during most of my remaining deployment. Based on the reports I received, I was not encouraged about his potential recovery.

I traveled from base to base, and the communications to back home weren't great, so it was hard for me to get information on JP. I soon ended up at a large base with a very good phone system and was excited to learn that I would finally get a chance to talk to him.

However, my excitement quickly turned back to hopelessness and discouragement. He was very weak, was just coming out of a coma and had lost some teeth; I could barely hear and understand him. It didn't sound like he was doing well at all. But there is always hope.

* * *

DEREK ANDRASIC WAS THE FIRST SERGEANT FOR THE 428TH Engineer Company. He made sure we were on top of our game: uniforms perfect, equipment cleaned and everything on our bodies was Army issued. The Army-issued sunglasses didn't work well for me, and I thought they looked ridiculous. We were told they were Army Tough, but I certainly didn't think so.

So instead of wearing those, I went online and bought some bullet resistant Oakleys that looked *way* cooler. They arrived two weeks later, and I put those babies on immediately! They were sleek and cool and felt good on my face. No one cared about this minor uniform infraction... no one except First Sergeant Andrasic.

"Lane! Take those sunglasses off! They are NOT Army issued!" he shouted at me.

Because I was 99% soldier, I replied, "Roger that, First Sergeant!"

And because I am 1% rebel, I pocketed them until I was out of sight, and put them back on when I got to my truck. My slight rebelliousness might have only turned into a funny anecdote, but it was those very sunglasses that protected my eyes from the shrapnel that flew through the truck during the explosion. They shattered into a million little pieces but kept my eyes intact and unharmed.

After the blast, Andrasic went back to the truck to search for a missing radio so he could account for all the equipment on the official record. No one else wanted to peer inside the truck and see—for lack of a better term—the "blood and guts" left behind, so Andrasic got stuck with the job. He later told me he saw chunks of my skin and bones splattered all over the cab, and my boot with my foot still in it, melted to the floorboard of the truck.

He said to himself, "I'll never see that kid again," believing I was a goner for sure.

6

BACK HOME

Dad's Account

The year 2011 was what my family referred to as "Our Year of Job." To fully understand just how significant that reference is, you first must understand that Job was an individual in the Bible that suffered many trials and tribulations throughout his lifetime.

Our trials began in 2008 and led up to the most difficult year in 2011. In January of 2008, my wife Kristi, Justin's stepmom, was rushed to the emergency room with a ruptured brain aneurysm. These are usually fatal; fewer than 25% of people survive.

As I stood by her bedside in the ER, the doctor looked at me and yelled, "What are you doing?! Get her children here! She's going to die!" Those words are forever engraved in my mind. All of our children were completely devastated at the high probability of losing their mom. Prayer became our only hope, and as we prayed, the bleeding miraculously stopped. In one small instant, everything changed direction. Plans for brain surgery began.

The doctors explained to me that even though the brain needs blood to function, blood *on* the brain—that is outside of where it is *supposed* to be—can be damaging. What Kristi was facing next was a traumatic brain injury (TBI).

The surgery was deemed a success, but Kristi still faced a long road of recovery, which included about six weeks of patient monitoring. Justin came up with the goofy idea to shave the letter "K" on the back of all the kids' heads in support of their mom. So Justin, Anthony and Eric did just that, but their sister Gina elected not to shave off her hair; I couldn't blame her considering she had such long, beautiful locks.

Kristi made it through this trial only to move to the next one, which proved to be even more difficult. Within a year, she started to have problems with her left leg. She would stumble and fall because her leg would give out while walking. One of these moments actually caused her to break her wrist. The doctors were focused on her recent brain surgery as a potential cause of the issue.

Yet, going through test after test, no answers had been found. The neurologist was stumped and referred us to the Mayo Clinic. Three months later and after countless CT scans, MRI's, spinal taps and nerve biopsies—the big "C" was found; Kristi had cancer! It was in her spinal fluid, which explains why finding it was so difficult.

The official diagnosis was Stage 4 Large B-Cell Lymphoma. Justin, Anthony, Gina, Eric and the entire family were once again faced with an unsure future for their mother. The doctors ordered chemo to begin as soon as we got back to Green Bay. Kristi's treatment involved a very aggressive, in-patient procedure with a high dose of methotrexate given through an IV.

The treatment plan called for her to be in the hospital for about five days every three weeks, which meant a lot of visits and hugs from our crew. Three months into treatment, she started losing the use of her right arm. Obviously this raised concerns, and doctors ordered an even stronger dose of the same medication. This was followed by more CT scans, MRI's and another nerve biopsy over the course of a year. Kristi's life was very difficult with cancer taking control. She, along with the rest of us, relied heavily on another big "C"—Christ. Our prayers were incessant and our love for God remained steadfast.

Treatment began showing results and that, in itself, was wonderful and encouraging news! Justin was deployed to Afghanistan in October of 2010, but religiously asked for updates on mom's condition. With one of the most dangerous jobs in the military, he had enough on his plate, so we didn't want to share anything that would cause him to lose focus on why he was there and the powerful work he was doing.

While deployed, soldiers are allowed a two-week break, and Justin chose to take his in February of 2011. He went to Puebla and Acapulco, Mexico. So, if I was going to see him, I had to go to Puebla.

Unfortunately, Kristi couldn't go because she was still sick after three years of battling with cancer. When I arrived, Justin was waiting at the airport for me. I wrapped him in a hug that I swear lasted ten minutes. I knew what he had been doing and how dangerous it was, so to see him safe and sound was overwhelming.

Fast forward a week—I had to get back to my wife and help her with our fight. At the airport, saying our goodbyes, I told Justin that I had a bad feeling about him going back. I told him to be smart and not to volunteer for anything extra. He looked me square in the eyes and said "Even if I lose my legs... I lose my legs. We will deal with it!" I now look back at that comment and it's mind blowing.

Back in Green Bay, Kristi's treatments were going well. So well, in fact, that her doctor was very confident that a stem cell transplant would be the next best course of action. It was the most effective way to kill the last bit of cancer and win this battle. A stem cell transplant is incredibly involved and requires the patient to stay in a "clean house" near Mayo Clinic.

We chose the Gift of Life house for Kristi's stay. It was the closest one to the clinic, which was great because there was lot of walking back and forth between the two. There were several patients staying there and most seemed to be having a rough go at it. They were wheelchair bound, could barely talk and were very weak.

Kristi was actually doing pretty well both physically and spiritually. We saw what cancer could be like, and we felt blessed that Kristi was hopefully on the way out from her battle. A caregiver was required to be with her around the clock, and I would be with her every other week; other friends and family members would fill in when I was back home running our business, Window World. Those that helped were her friend Judy, my daughter Sacha and even Kristi's older brother, Brian, from South Carolina was able to make the trip.

The stay at Gift of Life would be for at least six weeks depending on how she was doing. Physically, she was doing so well that we made a plan for a mini vacation to visit areas near Rochester and some of Minnesota. She had to wear a mask since her immune system was completely destroyed during the procedure; any little thing could get her sick. One day, I planned for us to visit a place that should be on everybody's bucket list: The Spam Museum.

Kristi's treatment was going so well that her doctor said she could go home a week early. "What a blessing!" I thought. When the doctors at Mayo gave her the news that she could go, I was back in Green Bay and her brother, Brian, was with her. It was Saturday, July 2nd. With such great news, I felt the need to celebrate. My way of celebrating good moments is by attending a car show, but this time I decided to enter the competition with my 1967 GTO. It couldn't have been a better experience—I placed first in my category!

Life finally seemed to be getting back on track, but little did we know it would once again derail with just one phone call. I got home around 3:00 p.m., and the phone immediately rang. It was the call a parent never wants to receive while their child is deployed. On the other end of the call was a lieutenant colonel telling me Justin had been hurt and was in serious condition. All he could tell me was that there was an IED blast and it blew up right under the driver's seat where Justin had been sitting. He asked me to try and stay close to my phone; he would call with updates as new information came in.

Kristi called soon after to inform me that they were an hour and a half from arriving home. I had to share the devastating news with her that Justin was in pretty rough shape. Justin's brother Anthony was visiting his mom and two half siblings in Ohio when I called with the news. Anthony later told me that he hung up completely in shock. He wandered back over to his family and just stared at everyone, struggling to find the right words.

As the calls came in, the list of injuries multiplied and grew worse. From the loss of a leg, and then his hand, and then his eye. The Army was doing the best they could with this information, but it didn't always get relayed as accurately as they wanted. The full extent of his injuries wasn't known yet and the information had to be passed down through many hands. The reality was that Justin was in really bad shape; they reported that he died twice, but they were able to bring him back.

The Army tries to get the severely injured back into the United States within seventy-two hours, but they weren't sure if they would be able to meet this goal because of the severity of his injuries. They were having a difficult time just keeping him stable.

As hard as all this was to hear, I knew how tough Justin was and how strong his faith was. If anyone could make it, it would be Justin.

The days that followed were unbelievably trying. It ended up taking over seven days to finally get him back to the U.S. During that entire time, I was waiting for the next call, or worse, the knock on our front door. I remember mowing the lawn and seeing a car that had government plates drive by the house. My heart dropped, but the car passed by. I thanked God it didn't turn into the driveway.

My family believes in a big God and it amazes me how the pieces of the puzzle so often fall into place. A close friend of mine, Bill, happened to have a cousin who was a military nurse. She was stationed at the very base in Germany that Justin was being flown to. She was able to find him in all the chaos and give us her personal view of his situation. That, more than anything, verified to us that God had Justin in his hands.

The call finally came in that Justin would arrive at Walter Reed Hospital within twenty-four hours. A plane ticket was waiting for me to fly there. Kristi couldn't go because of her compromised immune system. It would be dangerous for her to be near others in a hospital.

The Army had not been able to get in touch with Nadia, Justin's wife. He had inadvertently listed our number under her contact information when filling out his emergency data. Another barrier was that Nadia was in Mexico with her family, and I hadn't been in contact with her since he had deployed. It wasn't something I wanted to do, but I was asked to get in touch with her and relay the news.

When I finally called, Nadia's cousin, Adrian, answered the phone. I introduced myself and he told Nadia who was on the phone. She immediately began screaming over and over in the background, "No! No!"

Adrian yelled into the phone, "Is it true—is Justin dead?!" Then...click! The call dropped. In the urgency of the moment, I had forgotten that we had very poor phone reception in the house.

I quickly got in the car and drove to a high point and called again. Adrian answered again, and I could still hear Nadia screaming and crying. He asked me again, "Is it true? Is Justin dead?" I said, "No, no! He is still alive, but badly hurt."

Nadia had known something was wrong because they would Skype when the Internet at the base was available. When she didn't hear from him for a few days, she felt something wasn't right. Justin had mentioned to her about having to go out to "work" and that was the last she heard from him. So, when I was the next phone call she got, she knew that was not a good sign. I gave her all the information she needed so the Army could get her to Walter Reed as quickly as possible.

I arrived in Washington, D.C. at the hospital at the very moment Justin was being brought in. All I could see was my boy who wore his heart on his sleeve, who had so much positive energy, and had a vivid imagination, now lying there, busted up and torn to shreds in a coma.

It seemed like every machine ever made to keep someone alive was plugged into him. He was hooked up to a ventilation machine with a tracheotomy just to keep him breathing. He was connected to an EKG machine to monitor his heart in an effort to keep it under control. He had three separate wound vacs to help drain fluid that built up on each stump, and an incision that went all the way down his abdomen. A cooling vest was wrapped around him because his temperature kept spiking to a dangerous 106 degrees. A dialysis machine was also hooked up to his kidneys because one had shut down due to the shock of the explosion. Somewhere among all the technology, tubing and cords was my son, fighting for his life.

Nadia arrived at Walter Reed with her mom for support. I met her in the hallway and made an attempt to prepare her for what she was about to see. To be honest, nothing could prepare anyone for seeing a loved one ripped apart. We walked in together and were thrust into a very difficult scene. Her legs gave out, and I barely had time to catch her as she fell to the ground. As she cried, I held her just as anyone would have. Later, Nadia explained everything that she saw to her mom so that she could update the rest of the family back in Mexico.

Since Justin was in a coma, the doctors recommended we repeatedly tell him that he was safe at Walter Reed and no longer in Afghanistan. We were, of course, happy to oblige with the hopes that he heard and understood us. Though the staff was very attentive and caring in every way possible, there were times when they were brutally honest too. I was told that Justin's condition was about as bad as it could get when you considered all of the external and internal injuries he suffered. They said he had a fifty percent chance of surviving, and that the next few days would be crucial.

The surgeries began, and it seemed like every other day he had a procedure for a different part of him that needed reassembling. Now in addition to all the machines keeping him alive, he also had mechanical devices holding his bones in place called external fixators, "ex fix" for short.

The one positive note to any of this was that during all of these initial surgeries, Justin was still in a coma, leaving him essentially pain free. We knew if he awoke, he would certainly be suffering later, but for now it was a blessing that he was not aware of anything. On the flip side of that, a really big concern was that he wasn't aware of *anything*! A TBI could be permanent and vastly life changing. We were told that his TBI would be one of the biggest hurdles yet to overcome.

Nobody knew just how much brain damage was caused when Justin's head smashed into the four-inch thick, bulletproof windshield. Doctors explained that the brain would "pancake" inside the skull when subjected to that kind of force, causing it to slam into the sides of the skull. The brain damage may not be fully realized for weeks or longer. When you hear that sort of news, you can't help but think of all the "What if's" that could change his life forever, and the lives of those close to him.

We chose to take it one day at a time and try not to worry; we would cross that bridge when we got there. In the meantime, Justin still wasn't showing any signs of change or improvement, which only gave stronger evidence that he may not survive. With this thought in the forefront of my mind, it took me a few days to build up the courage to tell Justin something important. As a Christian, I felt the need to let him know that if God was calling him home, and he was fighting to stay, that it was okay to let go. When all you want as a parent is for him to wake up, that was a very difficult thing to say, but our God is a big God with bigger plans in store than our selfish minds can imagine.

I knew that patience had to be first and foremost for all of us because his progress and hopeful recovery was going to take time. In this type of situation, medical "baby steps" are to be celebrated. Unfortunately, the longer he was asleep, the more concerned I became. We could see all around us in the hospital soldiers who were progressing and doing really well. But some were not... and I would dwell on which one my son would be. I struggled with this, but I knew I would find the strength and courage to help him through whatever path God put him on.

Throughout the following days, Justin underwent many more surgeries and with each one we'd hoped he would open his eyes, but we had no such luck. One of the surgeries that concerned me the most was on his left leg. I was hoping that the doctors would be able to save his knee so that it would make using a prosthetic in the future much easier. Unfortunately, every surgery performed on that leg inevitably lead to failure; ultimately, the doctors decided to remove it. There wasn't enough solid bone or undamaged skin to close up the area around the stump.

This left only his femur, which was another great concern. I was able to see the x-rays on this portion of his leg and I counted seven separate breaks within a six to eight-inch space of bone. But the doctors were confident the bone would heal properly with the ex-fix holding everything in place. I disagreed and asked them if they thought a plate might be better instead, but they stuck with their choice. No one is perfect or infallible, and Justin would find out later that their decision was probably not the best one.

After close to five weeks, Justin finally opened his eyes! We were told that this could happen even though he was still not really all there. It's like the expression, "The lights are on, but nobody's home." I would try to say different things to get a reaction out of him, but I got nothing in response. I took this time to post on the Caring Bridge website to update everyone almost immediately, instead of calling 10,000 people and saying, "I just want my son back!" I had to constantly remind myself that baby steps forward were a positive thing.

Even with his eyes open, he was not showing any signs of acknowledgement. I desperately needed to know if he was there or not— I knew he couldn't talk, but at least a sign, a movement, *anything* would help at this point!

I reminded him of the goofy things he did as a child to see if I could get at least a smile. I spoke about the time when he was four and a flock of geese flew overhead. With a pretend shotgun, he started shooting and shouting, "BANG! BANG! BANG!" over and over. He must have gotten off thirty imaginary rounds. He turned to me and said, "I got three of 'em."

"That's it?" I responded. "After all those shots, all you got was three?" With a smile on his face, he said, "Yup." Thankfully, his aim got much better after undergoing Army training.

I talked to him about the time we were ice fishing on the pond behind my parents' house. My brother, Wayne, drilled about eight holes throughout the area and set top ups in each one. We caught four relatively fat, smallmouth bass, ranging from twelve to fourteen inches long. Justin was staring at the fish and then the hole in the ice, and I could tell that he was pondering something. I asked him, "What's wrong?"

In his innocent, yet very serious four year-old-voice he asked, "How do those big fish live in those little holes?" It hadn't occurred to him that we were standing on eight inches of thick ice that covered an entire pond.

Even after retelling Justin stories like these, there was still no reaction from him. This brought more concern for the mental well-being of my son. Another big problem, as if he needed more, was that as he was laid up in this hospital bed, he was quickly losing his strength. Up until this point, Justin had kept himself in pretty good shape, but now his once well-defined arms were slowly turning into toothpicks. His muscles were atrophying before our eyes.

One good sign was that as his body was mending, his kidneys finally started working, and his burns were slowly healing. He still stared into space a lot, which made the TBI issue still very real. Nevertheless, the fact that he was alive was nothing short of a miracle, but what kind of life would he have if he was trapped in his own mind? While my thoughts turned to situations like this, I could only sit by and watch him wither away and try to encourage him to keep fighting.

And then, the pinnacle moment we were all waiting and praying for finally happened! Many of the injured soldiers in the hospital received visitors that might stop by unannounced. This particular day, a two-star general chose to make his rounds in the intensive care unit where Justin was being treated. He placed a military coin in Justin's right hand and breaking military etiquette, came to attention and saluted Justin (normally, the lower ranking individual would salute first.) Then, to the surprise of everyone in the room, Justin raised his left arm, saluting him back! The entire room gasped at what we had just witnessed. There was not a dry eye in the place, including the general's, who responded with, "Once a soldier, always a soldier!" That moment gave us all a glimmer of hope that Justin was still in there and on his way back to us.

Being at Justin's bedside while he was recovering wasn't always the easiest thing to do. I became bitter, sometimes thinking that the Army flew us in to be his caregivers. We were doing things I thought I was finished with when Justin was a toddler. In accomplishing those daily tasks, we saw the burns, the scars and the long-term damage that would forever be a reminder of the tragic event that changed his life. Roaming around the hospital during my free time was very eye opening for me. I saw other soldiers with amputations that were much higher up, leaving it impossible to have children. Seeing this made me ponder if each soldier deployed to a war zone should bank a sperm donation, just in case they return unable to have children. This would provide each soldier the ability to still have children after their trauma, should they so choose.

All this time, Justin was physically improving, but he was still not fully aware of the seriousness of his injuries. And then one day, almost overnight, he truly "woke up." This is the moment the medical staff had warned us about... the moment the soldier becomes aware of what happened to him or her. When their new reality hits them like a brick wall. We were told that often they start to cry, completely freak out, or regress and seek solitude in their own minds for long periods of time. They told us that any number of reactions could occur, and that we needed to be prepared for anything. That day his tracheotomy was removed, and it was time to reveal to him the extent of his injuries. We had to tell him about his legs. He took a long look at what he saw and said, "Well, this is different!"

Those few words said so much more to us about his state than he could ever have imagined. They spoke acceptance, they spoke courage. Those words said, "I'm a soldier and will never give up the fight!" In that moment, the Rocky theme song started playing in my head.

Like I said, 2011 was "Our Year of Job." Continuing that theme, the year ended with my oldest son, Erik, and his wife, Jennifer, being in a very serious car accident on Christmas Eve. They were T-boned at seventy miles per hour and Jennifer was eight months pregnant. Thank God, all three survived, but Erik had broken a leg and was a little beat up. I believe that God knew Erik would be able to withstand the brunt of the impact, so he took the burden. That little unborn baby, Hayden, is now seven years old and perfectly healthy.

Job went through many trials and, through them all, he kept God first in his life—so much so that God blessed him with so much more than he ever had before. Job was given a very long life to enjoy all these new blessings.

Justin is equally blessed and is using his trials to bless those around him as he helps others find the courage to get through their own trials and tragedies.

He likes to tell people, "You can't kill a Lane." No matter how much the devil has tried, he hasn't won a fight in our family. We laugh at the attempts, but with God for us, who can be against us? With all that our family has been through, that seems to be an incredibly accurate statement. Never doubt that God has bigger plans for us all!

JUSTIN P. LANE

During Deployment 2010-2011 in Kandahar, Afghanistan

My RG-31 truck after being hit by a 200lb IED

64

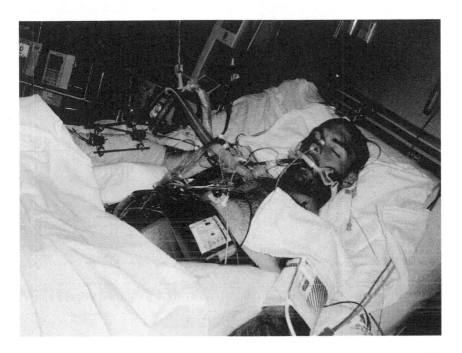

In a coma for 6 weeks at Walter Reed Hospital in Washington, D.C.

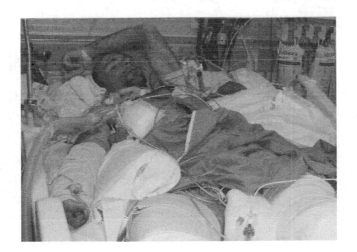

Woke up from my coma

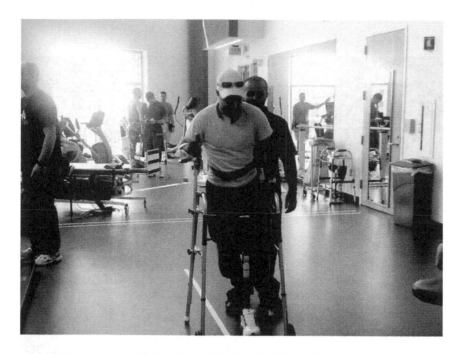

During therapy, I had to make the best of it.

Awarded a home by Helping a Hero with George P. Bush and Lee Greenwood on September 11th, 2014

My wife Crystal and I supporting Adapt-a-Vet

Singing in Houston, TX at Helping a Hero event with Gavin Degraw in December 2018

Went back to Afghanistan in April 2018 with Feherty's Troops First. Nice Try Taliban!

Inspiring is our Godly Purpose

7

BEDREST

Some people might think that lying around in bed all day sounds awesome, but I promise you, it most certainly was not.

In the time since I blacked out after the blast, I had been hauled from one hospital to another, before landing stateside at Walter Reed Army Medical Center in Washington, D.C. Walter Reed was the hospital designated as the first stop in the U.S. for wounded and ill soldiers. Since then, I had multiple blood transfusions, surgery after surgery—more than two dozen in all—and complication after complication.

I also died. Twice. By God's grace, the dedicated team of doctors and nurses in charge of my care were able to bring me back. Of course, I wasn't aware of any of this because I was in a coma for six weeks. Being in a coma and simply staying alive was, by far, the easiest part of what lay ahead of me.

I don't remember, but I was technically awake for a few days before I became *mentally* awake. This is a state called partial or minimal consciousness, where a person is coming out of a coma, but not quite with the program yet. It's a weird experience, to say the least. The nurses saw that I was coming around and called my family into the room.

My parents had been warned that I would be a little out of it because of the cocktail of pain medications pumping through my veins. They also warned my parents that most soldiers waking up in a situation like mine are scared and outraged and extremely disoriented. This makes perfect sense as the last thing they remember was being in a warzone, and now they are waking up in a hospital bed, connected to tubes and wires. I've even been told stories of soldiers screaming while trying to rip out their IVs and climb out of bed.

My response was different from the norm. My eyes opened slowly. I could barely move. I had a tracheostomy tube in my throat connected to a ventilator to help me breathe, so I couldn't speak. These things combined kept me still and quiet. I knew I was a different person than the one I had been before the bomb. I was changed but didn't know how. The doctors were frankly shocked I had woken up. They had told my family that the severe damage my brain had suffered would leave me unresponsive with mental issues, so they expected the worse.

Unable to speak, I couldn't tell my family that I was okay and that I was "here," but I knew that as long as I was in control of my ideas and the words running through my head, I would be okay.

My dad was the first face I remember seeing as I woke up. He was at my bedside, constantly wringing his hands and fraught with worry. It was tearing him up inside not knowing if I was okay, so he came up with a creative way to ask me. He wanted to test my brain, my eyes and my mental capacity. He didn't just ask, "Are you okay?" hoping I would nod. He found a sticky note and wrote, "Can you read this?" I nodded my head "yes." Tears streamed down his face as he hugged me as gently as he could, his face covered in an ear to ear grin. He tried to say my name but was too choked up for any words to come out.

Sobs of relief and tears of joy seemed to be the only language spoken as all of my family members came to see me. Nadia was there every day. It came as quite a shock to my family when they found out we had secretly married. My mom, Ann, was there as well as my siblings Ariann, Anthony, Sacha, Jacob, and Erik with his wife. Each got their turn to lean over my bed, say hello and give my shoulder a little squeeze or pat. Not many stayed long, but I understood why. No one wanted to see me in the broken and bruised state I was in. I couldn't blame them.

Soon, the doctors sat with me and told me about the twenty-six injuries I had sustained, the surgeries I underwent, and what they thought my future held.

Because of the location of the blast, my legs suffered the heaviest blow—my foot was left melded to the RG31. Both legs had to be amputated: the left just above the knee and the right just below. My four front teeth were knocked out and half of the middle finger on my right hand was cut off. My left femur was snapped in half.

More devastating, my pelvis was broken in half and had separated from my spine. Every organ inside of my body was shredded from shrapnel; the only ones not destroyed were my heart and left lung. In order to repair everything that was damaged, the doctors had cut me open from my chest to the bottom of my abdomen. Lastly, I had suffered a traumatic brain injury—one from which I was not expected to completely recover. But I had woken up, and that was the first step.

The doctors also told me I would never walk again. They said I wouldn't be able to use prosthetics because of the extent of the burns on my legs. They said I would be on medication my entire life. After my trach tube was removed, they said my speech would be affected, I would never be able to sing again, and I would talk funny because my vocal cords were damaged when they pulled it out. They said a lot of things.

Those first couple of weeks were filled with a lot of quiet hours, since a trach tube kept me from being the conversationalist I usually was. It was taken out after two weeks and I had to learn to talk in a very abnormal way. I had to block a little valve in my neck with my finger so the air in my lungs would pass over my vocal cords instead of coming out of the hole. It was painful and I could barely get out even a whisper.

I worked with a speech therapist and it took me several weeks to learn how to talk again. We worked through exercises with word pronunciation, and I would attempt to read simple phrases and sentences. It was quite frustrating at the beginning because my brain *knew* what I was trying to say, but my mouth wouldn't form the words. I was focused and determined to get it right! I wanted to speak again and to speak well. I wanted to return to singing harmony at church. I wanted to get back to as close of a "normal" life as possible.

Every waking moment was filled with pain upon pain. Simply lying in that hospital bed was torture on my broken body. Taking care of my body's needs often required the nurses tilting me over to one side, which was so incredibly painful I thought I might pass out. A scream would escape my lips almost every time, no matter how hard I tried to suppress it. It was certainly one of the most physically difficult times in my life.

* * *

ANYONE LYING IN A BED 24/7 FOR WEEKS AND MONTHS ARE PRONE to develop pressure ulcers, or bed sores, which begin when body parts covered by only a thin layer of skin, like the hips, elbows, or head, accumulate too much pressure from remaining in one position for too long. To stop this from happening, nurses turn the patient over to one side to give those pressure points a release.

One pressure ulcer formed on my buttocks from lack of movement in the bed. It was essentially a small hole forming in my skin. If left untreated, it could reach the bone and cause a serious infection.

While most professionals in the medical community think they are preventable, some think there could be situations where they are not. Either way, it was just one more issue to add to my list of ailments that had to heal before I could be released.

Anyone that has spent more than a day in a hospital bed knows how restless it can be. It felt like the walls were closing in and my room was turning into a prison cell. The monotony of it began to wear on me. The same food, same medications, same schedule. The nurses woke me every day at 4:30 a.m. for a blood draw and pain pills. Someone checked on me mid-morning to make sure I was still alive. After that there was lunch, more pain pills, then dinner. Occasionally the doctor in charge would come by to check my progress and break up the day. It wasn't a very exciting life... a far cry from my Army life of clearing IEDs and surviving the occasional blast.

Not only had I lost my legs and teeth, my muscle mass had now faded, along with my hope and will to live. I would have never even considered it before, but suicide was now a thought rolling around in my mind. I was no longer the man I used to be. I was no longer a man anyone could ever love. I was no longer a man with a purpose in this world. I kept all of these thoughts inside and never let anyone know what I was feeling. My family wasn't oblivious to my pain. They knew what I was going through physically, but I would never let them see the pain that was killing me emotionally.

* * *

WHILE I'VE HAD SHORT TERM MEMORY TROUBLE SINCE THE BLAST, there are two memories from my time at Walter Reed that are vivid for me. In 2011, there was an earthquake that shook the entire building. I gripped the rails of my hospital bed, thinking, "This is it. *This* is how I am going to die."

I survived living and working in a war zone, being blown up by an IED, and it was a dumb earthquake that was going to take me out. Fortunately, the shaking stopped, everything calmed down, and life went back to the new normal. It wasn't my time yet.

My second memory was of an elderly couple. I saw them walking the hallways from time to time, and soon they stopped by my room to say hello. The woman carried a basket of homemade cookies with her every visit and delivered a couple to every patient in my wing. The man always leaned slightly over my bed and knowingly said, "You're going to be all right. Everything will be okay." When he rose to leave, he finished with, "You will be out of here soon, walking on your own again."

This entire scene unfolded the same way, time and time again. Some days I would really try to listen to him with my heart and really believe what he was saying to me. Most of the time I ignored him and would often turn my head away when he was just trying to offer me comfort and hope.

But one day was different. The routine started out normally: the wife placed the cookies on my bedside table, and the man leaned over to repeat the same three lines I'd heard him say for weeks. I had had enough of his encouragement. I was tired of this guy telling me everything was going to be okay. Who was he, anyway?! He didn't know me and the limitations of my broken body. He didn't know the doctors were telling me I'd never live a normal life again. He didn't understand the physical pain and mental toll losing two legs takes on a man. I snapped.

I yelled at him, straight into his face, "You don't know my pain! You don't know how I feel!"

He could have yelled back...he should have walked away... he could have done a million other things to end that conversation. Instead, he very calmly took two steps back from my bed and rolled up his pants leg. He was wearing a prosthetic. I was shocked. This man should have put me in my place, but often with age comes a graceful, quiet patience. He took my anger and hopelessness and returned it with kindness and empathy. He didn't say a word; he didn't need to.

One simple gesture, raising his pant leg, let me know he *had* been exactly where I was. He didn't know me, but he *was* me, years ago. He knew the limitations of my body. He knew what the doctors were telling me. He knew the physical pain and mental anguish I was experiencing.

He had been right here once: the same broken and bruised man coming home from war less complete than when he had left. He had been in this bed, attached to these machines, feeling what I feel. After he left, I felt a weight lifted from me. His kindness and conviction, that I would heal, was my pain medication for the day. This man I didn't know had given me hope. He had shown me I was going to be all right. Everything was going to be okay. I would be getting out of here soon, walking on my own again.

* * *

DURING MY TIME THERE, WALTER REED WAS GOING THROUGH A transition to merge with Bethesda National Naval Medical Center. The staff was transferred to the other facility, along with all the equipment, supplies and medication. There was a period of time, maybe a day or two, where I would call for someone to help me move or ask for more pain pills or dinner, and no one would come. I thought they had forgotten about me, the wounded soldier who was missing his legs. How could I have been forgotten?

Finally, a doctor came to my room and apologized for the delay of care. Staff had been moving patients to the new location, and I was literally the last one left in the building. He asked me one question: "Where would you like to receive the rest of your treatment?" I had never thought about moving facilities, so he started rattling off a multitude of options nationwide. Then a thought stirred in my mind and I stopped him. I asked, "Where is the best place for prosthetics?"

He responded immediately with, "Brooke Army Medical Center, in San Antonio, Texas."

I chuckled, "Well, why didn't you say so? I want to go there." At least it would be warm, I thought to myself.

A general officer arrived to oversee my transfer. He handed me his challenge coin, something that isn't given out lightly, especially from a high-ranking officer to a junior enlisted soldier. It was a great sign of respect. He said it was something for my troubles.

After three months at Walter Reed, I was transported to Brooke Army Medical Center (BAMC) in a way that no civilian would ever experience—in a Lockheed C-130 Hercules military transport aircraft, the same model that flew me into Afghanistan not very long ago. All of the patients moving to BAMC were lined up on cots, hooked up to IV drips and monitors. I imagine this extra precious cargo made for an anxiety-filled transport for the pilots. I can picture them saying an extra prayer of protection over the plane, which was essentially a mobile hospital flying 30,000 feet in the air. They flew us safely into San Antonio and made a smooth landing at the airport.

My journey to recovery could recommence.

* * *

MY NEW ROOM WAS THE SAME OLD SCENE—SAME TUBES, SAME needles, same gown, same pain, just a different city.

"This sure is getting old," I thought to myself.

But one thing was new... I was getting a wheelchair. Sure, it wasn't new legs, but at least I would be able to get out of this hospital bed for a bit. I picked up moving in a wheelchair pretty quickly and had gotten good at maneuvering by the time Anthony came for a visit. We went for a stroll down the sidewalk outside of the building to get some fresh air.

Being the jokester and the oldest brother, I was looking to show him

I "still had it" and was still the same guy he'd known all his life. I cranked up the wheels and shot off down the sidewalk. I was flying fast when the small front wheels started to wobble. I took that as a warning and tried to slow down, but it was too late. The tires found a crack in the sidewalk and immediately slammed to a stop, but I kept going. I flew out of the wheelchair, landed on what was left of my wounded legs and fell flat on my face.

Pain flashed through my entire body as my face ground into the sidewalk. Anthony couldn't believe what had happened as he raced over to help me up. He dusted me off and set me back in my wheelchair. Now we are able to look back on that moment and laugh, but *man*, it sure hurt at the time! Needless to say, I found the need for speed a thing of the past.

Two weeks went by and I was barely settled into my new routine when a doctor came in with news. He had looked over my medical records and conferred with his colleagues.

"Unfortunately, we are not capable of handling such extensive spinal cord injuries such as yours at our facility," he said. "You're going to need a surgery that we can't provide, so we are going to transfer you to the Audie Murphy VA hospital here in San Antonio."

When my spine dislocated from my pelvis, it cut my nerves in half leaving my bowel and bladder lifeless. The only way for my body to remove waste was via a catheter and colostomy bag, which had been hooked up to me constantly since the blast. Unfortunately, the nerves were severed so greatly I would always have to use a catheter, but the good news was that the physicians at Audie Murphy could perform a surgery that would correct the part of the problem that required the colostomy bag.

The surgery was successful, and my colostomy bag was removed. The doctors wanted me to stay an additional month to make sure I was recovering well and did not develop an infection. During my stay, I started physical therapy to help get me "back on my feet."

For the first time, prosthetics for my legs were built. The physical therapist helped me put them on, thought they fit perfectly, and swung my legs over the side of the bed. I couldn't wait to take my first steps! It seemed like an eternity since I had walked on my own two legs. It was a weird sensation, standing up and feeling the weight of my body not on my feet but on my knees. I took a tentative step with my left leg, holding my hands out for balance. The therapist stood behind me, guiding my steps and hovering with his hands around my waist to catch me if I fell.

I felt some pain but was determined to keep going. I hauled my right leg forward, then left, then right, then left. The pain became too intense and I sat back down on the bed. The therapist took off my right prosthetic. The burned skin on my leg was torn and bleeding. My body wasn't ready yet. It was another crushing blow to my spirit, like a roller coaster of hope being given and taken away.

AFTER THREE OR FOUR MONTHS AT AUDIE MURPHY, IT WAS TIME to head back to BAMC. I visited the burn unit to learn how to take care of what remained of my legs. They needed to heal further and toughen up before I could even think about strapping on another pair of prosthetics.

While there is a lot to be said for modern medicine, I found the best treatment for my burns was aloe vera. I would snap the end off one of the leaves and rub the gel on my burns. After about a week or so doing this, I was amazed at how much they had healed. My skin had changed to a healthier pink and felt much stronger when I touched it. It was finally time for the prosthetics! Or so I thought...

My burns were deemed "healed" and I was transferred once again to a facility located on BAMC called the Center for the Intrepid (CFI). It is a rehab center for both amputees and burn victims that teaches patients how to perform everyday tasks wearing prosthetics and gets them ready for reintegration into the world. It's a beautiful, round modern building filled with exercise equipment, pools and integrative technology designed to get us on our feet again, figuratively and literally.

Directly behind the CFI are the Fisher Houses, which is lodging for family members and their soldiers undergoing therapy. This was a good design, stationing all the soldiers here together... it allowed us to meet brothers and sisters-in-arms with similar obstacles to overcome. We swapped stories, woes and concerns, which all helped with the mental healing process. We were in this together, just like we were before out there on the battleground.

As therapy started in the CFI, I mistakenly thought I could just slap on prosthetics and zip across the room. I couldn't *wait* to get out of my confining wheelchair. What I didn't realize was how much muscle mass I had lost. I went from being a built, tough soldier with washboard abs to a limp, skinny mess of bones, minus two legs. Luckily, powering the wheelchair kept my lungs somewhat in shape, but I still felt winded because of my lack of daily physical activity.

To this day I still proclaim that my therapist, Fred, is the toughest therapist to ever walk the face of the earth. He had me doing core exercises I had never done before, not even in basic training. To be able to use prosthetic legs, your core has to be twice as strong to lift them. My therapist walked me through a number of movements to stretch my muscles that had become almost excruciatingly tight during the year I spent lying in a hospital bed.

I slowly started to rebuild my muscles, and I became more active. New prosthetics were made for me and I couldn't wait to try them out. We hooked them on, and I stood up. I started moving forward: left foot, right foot, left foot, SNAP! My leg buckled beneath my weight. I immediately knew what it was. A few weeks prior at a doctor's appointment, we had discussed the integrity of my left femur. They confirmed it was healed and ready for the use of a prosthetic. And it *was* ... for two steps.

I looked up at Fred. "Did you hear that loud pop?" I asked.

"No," he replied, probably used to patients not wanting to work as hard as he deemed necessary. "Keep walking."

I reached for my aching leg. "Fred, it hurts to walk on it," I explained. "I think I broke my femur." I sat down to relieve some of the pain.

"Fine," he relented. "Go get it checked and then come back and finish your therapy." He helped me back into my wheelchair and I rolled down the emergency department, feeling broken yet once again.

I've always heard the statement "No one knows your body better than you" and in this case, that proved true. I snapped my femur in half once again. It may have looked healed in the x-rays, but it wasn't. Almost immediately, I was taken down to surgery. Fred and his therapy would have to wait. This time, the surgeon screwed a plate into my bone to keep it together. As soon as the incision healed, I could try the prosthetics again. I remembered my secret weapon... the aloe vera plant sitting on a window ledge in my room.

About a week later, at the one-year anniversary of losing my legs, I was ready to give walking another try. Baby steps, I reminded myself.

This time, as I took my first steps (again), nothing bled, nothing snapped, and there was minimal discomfort. I worked hard with Fred and did every little exercise, stretch and movement he told me to. Soon enough I was up and walking. Sure, I was moving around with the assistance of a walker, but I was up!

I may have looked like a crippled soldier shuffling around like an old man, but I didn't care *what* I looked like. It was me and my two legs. I felt proud, accomplished and taller. In fact, I WAS taller. The prosthetics moved me from five foot six to five foot seven.

Bedrest was now a thing of the past.

8

MY NEW NORMAL

S tep one was complete: I was out of the hospital bed and walking on my own with my prosthetics!

Now it was time for personal growth. I was still in the Army and I was offered a thirty-day vacation after everything I had gone through. Family was the first thing on my mind, so I chose Wisconsin. I needed some sense of normalcy in my life after everything I had been through, and I knew being back with my family was the best thing for me. I needed to get away from medical facilities and physical therapy and hospital food.

Things with Nadia had deteriorated, as many soldiers' relationships and marriages tend to do. I had learned she was unfaithful to me while I was going through therapy. We decided to call it quits about the time I got my prosthetics, after two years and six months of marriage. I was trying to learn to walk again and build my confidence both physically and emotionally; being in our marriage was not helping. We parted ways and went in opposite directions to live our own lives.

Trying to distance myself from her led to more stress, anger and thoughts of suicide. The path our relationship had taken was out of my control, and I didn't like it. What had I done wrong that led her to cheating? I had tried to be a good husband to her, but I know being gone didn't help. What did I do to deserve this life I was being handed? First the blast and the loss of my legs, and now my marriage?

My thoughts turned even more to self-pity. Who would ever want to be with me like this, half a man? No one could ever love me. I would be alone forever. My life was whirling out of control. I felt like I would never be able to escape this deep depression.

I spent most every night trying to decide the best way to kill myself. Overdosing on painkillers or slicing my wrist felt like the easiest way out. I even bought a gun, thinking that would be the best way to end my life, much surer and faster than pills or slowly bleeding out.

Every fiber of my being was screaming, "Just end it!!" I wanted to end the pain and leave this world of hurt, disappointment and despair. I came close to committing suicide, but God had bigger plans for me. He was the reason that I could never quite pull the trigger, or finish an entire bottle of pills, or press the knife deeper into my skin.

I didn't understand this at the time, but I have come to realize that God will never put me through something I can't handle. He was there with me, right by my side, through it all. From the days of living with my mother heating up a can of Beefaroni for my brother and I, to making it through the rigors of basic training, to being blown up by an IED in the RG31, to lying in a coma in the hospital bed, to learning how to walk on new legs.

He was with me then and he is with me now. My thoughts of self-pity and suicide started to fade during the flight on a private jet from San Antonio to Green Bay, courtesy of Veterans Airlift Command (VAC). The VAC is an all-volunteer organization that gives free flights to post-9/11 soldiers who were wounded in battle; they also provide flights for wounded soldiers' families. Amazing men and women across the nation give their time and their aircrafts to fly injured soldiers where they need to go.

My dad had told me news outlets would be waiting when I arrived in Wisconsin, and I had a scheduled interview with Rachel Manek from Fox 11 News. We landed after a smooth flight, and I stepped off the plane into a flurry of excitement and emotion. It seemed every news station within the surrounding Green Bay area was there to get my story. They all wanted a piece of me for what they dubbed "Justin's Journey." It was a very nerve-wracking experience. I was used to being behind a .50-caliber rifle, not in front of a news camera.

Every time I visited home, the news stations would interview me and record what I had been up to. After answering some questions about my stint in the Army, the blast that injured me, and my recovery thus far, I headed to my father's house. There is an old saying along the lines of: "There's nothing quite like going home."

For me, this never rang truer than on this trip. I relaxed at home, vegging out with my dad on the couch. I attended services at the church where I grew up. I caught up with some buddies from the 428th Engineer Company. The dark cloud swirling in my head finally started to clear. I felt the weight of depression lifting from my spirit.

My month off flew by. I was soon boarding another plane and headed back to San Antonio to finish my therapy. I still had a lot to learn. I spent my days maneuvering in tight areas in a wheelchair, cooking, washing dishes, showering and completing many other household chores. But the best item on the checklist was driving. I had to learn how to drive with prosthetics and an adaptive driving kit that allowed me to reach the gas and brake without the use of feet. It consisted of a metal handlebar that connected to the dash that I pushed and pulled for the brake and gas pedals.

It was new and challenging, driving only with my hands, and surprisingly very fun! It only took me one lesson to get the hang of it. The instructor even commented that she had never seen anyone drive so well on their first trip out of the gate. I parked the car and switched off the ignition, then she said, "Want to go take your driver's test?"

I exclaimed, "Of course! Let's go!" I passed with flying colors and was handed a shiny, new driver's license. I was elated that I didn't have to rely on someone else to drive me around. I felt complete freedom. Having that feeling come back put me on top of the world.

Soon after, my brother Anthony decided to move to San Antonio. He said he was going to help me out and take care of anything I might need, but anyone who is a big brother knows that it's always going to be the other way around. But hey, maybe I'd let Anthony heat up SpaghettiOs for me.

We rented house together and it felt like the good old days being under the same roof again. We played arcade games at Dave and Buster's and scoped out new restaurants to see if they were potential date spots for future girlfriends. Anthony applied to the San Antonio Police Academy and graduated to become a full-fledged member of the police force. Seeing him grow up and become a responsible, successful adult has been one of the best parts of my life. We had a rocky time as kids, and we could have ended up in very different places. I was as proud as a big brother could be.

In 2013 I was still in the Army, but about to medically retire—once the mounds of paperwork went through. I was once again standing on a precipice, trying to choose what I was going to do with the rest of my life.

At first I thought it was a life in Mexico teaching, then I committed my entire life to the Army... now what?

Technically, I could stay in the Army as a combat engineer and spend my days doing what I had been trained to do—sniffing out IEDs with my team. With the revenge I wanted and hatred that I felt for the Taliban, this seemed like a viable option. I could return to Afghanistan and finish my fight. I took a few days to consider it but, ultimately, I decided against that choice. I figured my dad would kill me before the Taliban did. He had been through what no parent should ever have to experience. If I told him I was going back overseas, I was certain he'd have a heart attack or lock me up in his basement. At the very least, he would not be happy with my decision. And that seemed to be the general consensus.

Everyone I spoke with about the possibility of me staying in the Army had one thing to say: "You've already given enough for your country."

Perhaps. In the end, I knew I could still give more to our beautiful nation as a soldier, but I also knew it was time to return to my family and focus on myself and my new hopes for the future.

So, what other options were out there? I looked at both government jobs and civilian jobs, some with pretty decent looking salaries, but the thought of being tied to a desk all day after I had been lying in a hospital bed for a year didn't strike me as ideal or amusing.

I was in a bed and a wheelchair for way too long, and I didn't get these amazing prosthetics to sit around on my butt all day. I wanted to get up and move! I was no further along in my search for careers than when I started, but God had already chosen a new career path for me.

9

A CAR RIDE WITH GOD

I always enjoy seeing the different reactions I get when I tell people, "I heard God's voice." You can tell a lot from the expressions on their faces. How they respond to this statement gives me a glimpse into their own heart and mind.

If someone reacts with joy or amazement or empathy, I could assume they have a personal relationship with God. If someone scrunches up their face with the look of disbelief or one of slight contempt, I would assume they are a non-believer or perhaps that they *do* believe but have anger or other issues toward him.

I have certainly related to all of the above thoughts and emotions at some point during my spiritual walk. After waking up from a coma to see an ugly, broken, wreck of a man staring back at me from the mirror, you'd better believe I had a bone to pick with God. I had moments of sheer frustration, moments when I would simply shake my head in disbelief at the lot I had been given in life thus far, and plenty of moments of yelling at him in anger.

There were a multitude of questions I needed answered. I thought that losing my legs, one complaint among my laundry list of other medical issues, was a punishment for something I had done wrong in my life.

I would think it true that most people have those same thoughts at least once in their lives when they are going through dark times: Why me? What did I do to deserve this?

But my hope is that I can be a small beacon of light to help guide you out of your tunnel of despair, hate, anger, depression or whatever it may be.

God is always with you! He was here with me when I sat and wrote this book, and he is here with you now as you read it.

It took me well into adulthood (and not to mention being blown up) to figure this out, but I have learned at least one truth in this life: I did *not* get injured in that blast because I had done something wrong.

As a child, my father would watch me do something wrong and then punish me for my mistakes. What I didn't understand then was that the punishment was to help me learn from my mistakes and grow into a better person with a knowledge between right and wrong, and the wisdom to make the right decisions. My dad wasn't hovering over my shoulders waiting to catch me messing up so he could immediately dole out a punishment, and neither is God. God is by your side so when those moments occur, he can pick you up, stand you on your feet, brush you off and point you in the right direction.

He calls that *grace*.

I didn't lose my legs because of all the wrongs that had I accumulated in my life. I lost them because I drove over an IED that a terrorist had placed in that specific spot at a specific moment in time.

Now, we are faced with the inevitable question every person is sure to ask in this circumstance: "If God is so good and gracious, why did he let me hit the IED in the first place and go through all the pain and suffering that brought me to this moment?"

My response is this: It happened because God has given us one important, little thing—free will.

I *chose* to become a soldier.

I *chose* to be a combat engineer.

I *chose* to be on that mission.

I even *chose* to drive the truck.

Instead of plotting out our entire lives ahead of time, God allows us to choose our paths. He follows along, watching our every move and guiding us in the best direction, if we choose to listen. And in moments when we need him, like for instance, when we are blown up by an IED in Afghanistan, we can call upon him for help; our father in heaven is there to answer.

I came to this realization after what I now call "my ride with God." I had completed all of the required surgeries and therapies, and I had relearned how to drive. Since I had passed my driving test for the second time in my life, I treated myself to a sporty Nissan 370Z. It was time to continue my personal growth. God and I had some business to attend to.

Every day since the blast had funneled me further into darkness and despair. My marriage was over, my legs were gone, my chosen career had ended. The daily painkillers I was on were affecting my mind, and many everyday tasks were still a chore for me. I had many questions, but no answers.

I thought a ride in my shiny, new car might be good medicine. As soon as I pulled out of the drive, I began a conversation with God. I say conversation, but what happened was a lot of yelling and questioning that turned into calm reflection and perhaps a few tears. I had a *huge* list of "why's" I was trying to talk through. Anyone passing me on the road was sure to wonder who the crazy guy having a lengthy conversation with himself was.

I was cruising down the highway, listening to rap music because that's what the cool kids do when driving their sports cars. Completely exhausted from my long, one-sided conversation with God, I shouted one final question: "What do you want me to do with my life NOW?"

I took a deep breath and finally shut my mouth to give God a chance to respond. And he took the opportunity I gave him.

Jay-Z was rapping about ten chains but was cut off mid-chorus. The station flipped to a Christian music station. Weird. I hadn't touched the dials, and this was a new car, so it shouldn't be malfunctioning. What had just happened?

Wait... was this God answering?

I couldn't believe it. He had my attention now. A song was just starting, so I paid close attention.

"Another day, another fight,
it always feels like an uphill climb
Another step, another mile,
the story of your life."

Every cell in my body snapped to attention. I kept listening...

"It's harder than you ever thought,
and it costs you everything you've got
When your back's against the wall
and you feel like giving up."

This song was for me. I knew God had a hand in it. The chorus began to play...

"This is only a mountain;
you don't have to find your way around it.
Tell it to move, it will move.
Tell it to fall, it will fall."

"Yes, Lord!" I cried. My situation is only a mountain; I can get past it. I can move past my broken body, my failed marriage, the complete upheaval of my life and be who he has called me to be!

With new thoughts racing through my mind, I decided that I would *not* let people see me as some poor kid who lost his legs in the war. I would *not* let people feel bad for me and I would *not* feel sorry for myself.

No! If anything, the Army had taught me to be strong, to never give up, to never surrender.

By the time the song ended, tears were streaming down my face. Then the DJ announced the artist's name: Jason Castro. I later learned he had just earned a fourth-place finish on American Idol. He had written the song that healed my brokenness, "Only a Mountain."

After this song, my mind was racing. Then I heard God's voice: "Get a guitar and start playing."

I was certainly surprised, but then realized that God knew me quite well. He knew the biggest passion of my heart. I'd loved music since I was a kid, jamming out to the classics with my dad and Anthony and hitting the music stores to get the newest CDs the day they released. I had played drums since I could remember. It seemed that now God was calling me to use the gift he had previously given me.

I stopped right there in the middle of the highway, pulled over to the side of the road, and typed "guitar stores" into my GPS. It pointed me to the closest one, and I started driving. I picked out a guitar, a microphone, an amplifier, cables and anything else I thought I might need. No, I was not a guitarist, never had been, but I had a rhythm in my head and a soul filled with music. Obviously, the first song I wanted to learn to play was "Only a Mountain."

After all, it was the song I credited with saving my life. As I unloaded all my new purchases into the living room, excitement filled my veins with a sense of something to accomplish ahead of me. I learned the chords, strum pattern and lyrics before I hit the pillowcase that night.

I couldn't believe it—I was about to have *fun* with music! I finally felt like I had something to look forward to. It felt like God was giving music back to me. I thought it would simply be a new form of therapy to help me through my daily struggles, but God had something a little bigger in mind.

After only a few months of practicing, I started to feel pretty good about my ability. I thought it might be time to share my love of music and spread my joy to others. What if I could record my own version of "Only a Mountain"? I searched online for "best recording studios in San Antonio" and Chris Lieck Studios popped up. I called and spoke with Chris, the owner.

"Hello, sir," I started. "My name is Justin Lane. I am a double amputee soldier."

"Hi, Justin," he interjected. I continued, "I am wanting to record a song and make a video for my YouTube channel."

For those of you that don't know, Chris is a rock star from Hollywood who was discovered playing the drums when he was seven.

He opened his first publishing company at age seventeen. His labels have produced platinum records and have earned Grammy and Billboard Awards. He asked, "What instruments do you play?"

"I am currently learning the guitar and I played drums for fourteen years before I was injured," I answered. I paused, then added, "And I can play 'London Bridge is Falling Down' on the piano." I chuckled to myself.

Chris was not as amused, but he scheduled a session with me anyway.

Walking into his multi-million-dollar studio, I wondered what I might be getting myself into. It was an amazing setup filled with individual recording booths, innovative sound equipment and expensive instruments. I was feeling a little intimidated and certainly out of my element.

Chris wanted to see if I was serious about my music and vocals, so he ran me through a twenty-minute session of vocal exercises. When we were done, he commented, "Wow. I am very surprised."

I was confused. "Why is that?" I asked.

"Because you said you were a drummer," he laughed enthusiastically. "I thought you would suck."

I chuckled and asked, "Well, how did I do?"

He said I passed his test better than ninety-five percent of his students. "Your voice is very well put together," he said. It felt good to have a professional in the music industry compliment me in such a way, especially after my doctors told me I would have speech issues for the rest of my life and would never be able to sing again.

All that work with the speech therapist had paid off! Chris penciled me in on his calendar for a few days to come in and record. I walked out of the studio with my head held high, feeling tremendous pride about how far I had come and my abilities thus far. It was a feeling I hadn't experienced in quite some time.

God has an amazing way of turning your life around without you even knowing it, even before you realize you *need* to be turned around. It's so reassuring to know that the God watching over us *wants* the best for each and every one of us.

But as humans, we think too small. God thinks *bigger*. I thought music was just going to be a therapeutic tool, another step in my healing process, but God knew it could be much bigger than that. While I was lying in my bed dreaming that night, God was cooking up something amazing to pour into my life.

My dreams were about to become a reality.

10

STEPPING UP FRONT

I had spent my teenage and young adult years as a drummer for a few different garage bands, halfway hiding toward the back of the stage. It felt good there. I wasn't the face of the band. I wasn't putting myself out there like the lead singer was. The desire to be a lead singer was never something I had experienced. Being a drummer suited my personality; I could do my thing on the drums and still remain a little bit out of the main scene.

But if I have come to learn anything, it's that God likes to move us out of our comfort zones. He'll change up your scenery when you least expect it. He wants to challenge you to help you grow as a person in his creation, and he often does this by putting you in spots you never thought you would be in.

My first day in the recording studio had arrived. It was time to put my drumming skills, guitar strumming and singing voice to the test. We were ready to put together a video that might inspire others. Chris greeted me at the door, excited to get started on our day. He set me up for the guitar part first.

I sat in a chair, propped up my new guitar, took a deep breath, and began playing when I got the cue. My fingers sailed through the chords as I played through the song for the first time. The piano part came next, and I struck each key in perfect rhythm, which was a feat in itself because I had only recently learned how to play. Chris had been teaching me as we recorded. The next couple of days were a whirlwind of playing each instrument's part, singing the verses and chorus, then starting all over again. If I messed up, I started over. Sometimes this was Chris's call, but mostly it was mine. I recorded double tracks for the bass and the electric guitar. The only part left to record was the drums.

Chris turned to me and said, "Justin, I can bring someone in for this. I know a drummer that would be willing to come in and record it for us."

I looked down at my prosthetics and I thought about it briefly, but I already knew this was something I wanted to see through on my own. I *was* a drummer, after all. I had played every other part; I could do this too. I answered Chris proudly, "I got this."

I climbed behind the drum kit and picked up a pair of sticks. It had been so long since I had sat in this seat. I ran the smooth hickory of the drumsticks through my fingertips, trying to remember the last time I had played. I gave the one in my right hand a quick twirl. My heart was beating a little faster.

The lyrics of the song were sprinting through my head...

"It's only a mountain
Tell it to move,
It'll move."

I thought about all of the mountains that I had faced since the blast. I thought about all the future mountains yet to pop up in my way. Then I thought about all of the goals I had set for myself, right there on the other side of the mountain. "Move mountain," I thought to myself. "All right," I said to Chris as I looked up at him, "Let's do this."

After we got the vocals, guitar, drums and piano tracks laid down, we got to work on making the video. Chris trained the camera on me as I ran through the song on each instrument once again. It felt weird, this camera following my every move, but the thrill of being behind the drums again, not to mention the guitars I had just learned, was amazing. It felt familiar. Normal, even. Like home.

With the video and audio recording on file, we started to edit. This was the last part and, for me, the most tedious part of the whole process. Chris and I sat together and decided where slices of me playing the drums and guitar would go and when we needed to move from one instrument to the next.

We pulled a few pictures from my photo albums to include. There's one of me in the hospital bed surrounded by my fellow Army riffraff. Included in the picture is Staff Sergeant Ratliff, Sergeant Bowden, Specialist "Doc" Warren, and Specialist "Doc" Wright. There's a shot of me when I was first able to walk in my prosthetics with ease and another of me climbing a rock wall at the Center for the Intrepid.

I recorded a short message at the end about why I was making the video. I was extremely nervous filming it with the camera pointed right at me, from my head to my prosthetic feet. I hadn't written anything out and this was my first time to really speak about what had happened to me. I was trying to speak from my heart to the heart of any hurting person who might watch it, whether it be a situation similar to mine or something completely different.

It was finally finished: my very first music video! I had played six instruments on my own. Looking back now I can see a few things I would like to change—move to a drum shot here, a chord I could have played better, maybe a fuller storyline. I definitely feel like my singing voice has improved. Overall, I am still very happy with my music and proud of what I did... that I had the courage to do it in the first place!

I decided to go by JP Lane (my middle name is Patrick) as an artist since there were already a lot of Justins in the music scene. I uploaded the video to YouTube and my social media outlets. My goal was to inspire others with what I have been through, and the fact that I overcame it, just as they could overcome whatever was hampering them in their own lives. I hoped that people would share my video and story with their friends and family that were hurting or going through a difficult time.

One of the best ways to spread joy is through music—that was my plan. I did not begin my music journey with the intent to get noticed or to become famous or to make money. In my heart of hearts, I yearned to spread a message of hope and joy, and the ability to overcome. After about a week on YouTube, my video had racked up a whopping 200 views!

Thanks, Dad!

* * *

ONE COMPONENT I HAD NOT THOUGHT ABOUT WAS DEVISING A plan to get my message out there. I decided to pay to promote my video, and that raised views a bit, but not a huge amount. Nonetheless, within a week, I got an interesting call.

"Is this JP Lane?" the official sounding person on the other end of the line asked.

"This is," I replied. The woman continued, "We would like you to sing your version of 'Only a Mountain' at the Presidential Inauguration for Barack Obama this January 20th, 2013."

An audible scoff escaped my mouth. "Uhh, I think you have the wrong JP Lane," I quickly said with an amused chuckle.

The woman responded, "You *are* the double amputee that recorded a version of 'Only a Mountain,' are you not?"

Wow. She really *was* looking for me! I sat up straighter. "Yes, that's me. But I've only been playing the guitar for a couple of months," I confessed.

"That's okay," she replied. "We would like you to talk a little bit about your story and then sing that song."

I was dumbfounded. Awestruck. In denial. How was this possible?! How was I, Justin Lane, being invited to perform at one of the nation's biggest events? Moreover, it only happens every four years, so I'm sure the competition for a performing spot is highly sought after. I quietly and humbly accepted the offer and hung up the phone.

Wounded vets such as me often become distant and reserved. They lose their confidence, become shy even. This was certainly the case for me at the beginning of my new life without complete legs, but after a while, I started giving things over to the Lord.

I would never get my legs back—give it to God.

I would always be disabled—give it to God.

I can't sing live in front of one million people—give it to God.

Like I said before, I was a drummer. I hid in the back of the stage. But with every day that passed by, God restored my confidence and I allowed him to push me to the center stage, quite literally. I couldn't possibly have been more front and center than performing my first-ever live show in Washington D.C., playing on a stage in front of all those loving American people waving their flags and cheering for me.

I arrived in D.C. the evening before the inauguration. I met up with my parents and their spouses for dinner. We spent the next day visiting all the tourist attractions, including Arlington National Cemetery. I found the headstone for Justin Ross, my friend who had been killed by the sniper. It was standing in the large field, in line with the headstones of so many fallen soldiers. So many killed.

So many families left grieving. It was hard to breathe, standing in that cemetery among so many that had given their lives for our country. I spent a little time talking to him, catching him up on all that had happened since he had been killed in action. I said a prayer for his family and left.

In the afternoon I hung around the hotel lobby with my family, jamming out on my guitar, trying to calm my nerves. When it was time, I headed over to the stages. I was nervous, but more excited to get up there and play for the crowd. At about seven o'clock, I took the stage in my uniform. Four marines marched in perfect unison down the aisle carrying the flags. There was complete silence. I raised my microphone and sang the national anthem acapella. I was thankful that I didn't screw up any of the words as we have seen others unfortunately do so many times in the past. Whew!

About 9:30 p.m., I played "Only a Mountain" in front of a crowd at the Black Tie and Boots Ball. I flew home the next morning feeling on top of the world. Singing at the inauguration gave me a new confidence —a new pep in my step, and now I was hungry for more!

* * *

I logged in to check out my video and it had boomed from a few hundred views to over 30,000! I was stunned! It felt too insane to be real. I had inspired enough people, or at least made them interested in my story, to want more. Now traffic was flowing through my YouTube channel and my message could be spread to those who needed to hear a voice of hope. I was walking on cloud nine, but it's often during these happy, elated moments when the world likes to knock you down a peg or two.

I started reading the comments under my video, which was a mistake. The majority of them were overwhelmingly kind and encouraging, and many people expressed a feeling of togetherness and compassion. Some posted about their own time in the military. Others just offered a quick, "Good job, man!" or "Thank you for sharing!"

And then I found one that tried to destroy all of the happiness I had felt in that moment: "Look, you all praise him just because he's crippled... He has no talent at all."

My spirit sank. I was crushed. I fell hard from cloud nine and smacked back down to earth. All of the confidence I had just gained—learning to walk and drive again, learning to play guitar, tackling those drums with my own two legs, racking up 30,000 YouTube hits, being asked to sing at a presidential inauguration for Pete's sake—all of that was ripped away by a lone, mean spirited comment.

So, I do what many kids do when they are feeling low—I called my dad. He said to brush it off, remain strong and not reply. He knew someone else would "take care of it."

Sure enough, fans of my video and my story came to the rescue with replies that set this guy straight. Knowing that strangers had my back like that really lifted me up. They stood up for what was right in their eyes and showed common courtesy and respect. I could never thank them enough.

I know there will always be those people whose sole mission in life is to bring others down. They are negative, hateful and mean. They are also the ones we need to pray for God to do a great work in their lives. I will never again let one mean-spirited person bring me down and ruin the path I am traveling.

My life took a short breather from the exciting flurry of recent events as I regained my foothold and pushed forward through the negative.

The next step was expanding my portfolio of songs. I've always enjoyed most genres, so I learned a little pop, funk, country and a handful of others. I didn't have a clear direction, and this was a misstep on my part. Anytime you start down a new career path, the most important thing you can do is have a serious talk with yourself to figure out what direction you need to go and to make some small goals that will ultimately lead to your one big one. I didn't do this, and it cost me a lot of time and money.

First, I started performing cover songs for free, taking requests online and posting the videos to my YouTube channel. I thought this would help me to gain a little exposure. I formed a band without really stopping to ask God what he wanted me to do. We got a handful of bookings at small venues for even smaller amounts of money. I would often forego payment so I could make sure my band members were taken care of. We played cover song after cover song in restaurants and small dives. They would offer piddly amounts of money because they knew we were new in town and needed the work. We got next to nothing for our time. I started to feel like my talents and that of the other band members were being taken advantage of, even wasted.

What I didn't stop to think about was God's plan in all of this. After all, he is the one that set me upon this course. Shouldn't he be the one that was driving? God knows the value of each and every one of us, and he knew the value of me and my bandmates. That is the reason I should have paused and listened to what he had to say and for his direction.

I decided, when I first started out, that I would keep my music clean. I felt like God was telling me that as long as I stuck to who I was in my heart, any audience I might play for would be able to see God through me and my testimony, whether I was singing a love song or a ballad about my dog. I was certainly doubtful, anyone would be... not many of the popular artists out there manage to keep their music family friendly, but I made a commitment and stuck with it—and it would pay off. I felt God's tug on my heart a few months later.

* * *

THE BOSTON MARATHON BOMBING IN APRIL OF 2013 WAS ONE OF those events that shook the whole nation. When such a wonderful, prestigious event beloved by many is shattered in such a way, people come together for the greater good.

My brother Anthony and I were watching the news coverage at the time, and I felt the need to spend time with those that were injured. I voiced my thoughts aloud to Anthony and immediately felt God's voice saying, "That's great, but wait two weeks."

"Why do I need to wait two weeks?!" I wondered.

God responded, "They need time to heal."

Okay, then, I will wait. I dived into fundraising to finance the trip. I posted a note on Facebook about wanting to make the trip to Boston and by the next morning, I had the funds for a plane ticket. *"Well, that was easy!"* I thought. God provided so quickly, I decided to invite some other warriors to travel with me. We totaled four in all: Michael, Zedrick, Lee and me.

The whole trip ended up being paid for, thank God! Friends, family and anonymous supporters contributed all the money we would need for the trip. We packed our bags, landed at Logan Airport in Boston and checked into our hotel.

The following morning, we went to the Spaulding Rehabilitation Hospital. We didn't have a point of contact at the hospital; we were just hoping to get to meet some of the injured.

Unfortunately, we couldn't work anything out that day, but the staff set us up for visiting the next day. We met with about four or five of the injured and their families. I performed "Only a Mountain" once more and we all shared our stories with each other. There was not a dry eye in the hospital by the time we left.

They thanked us for coming and said we were the best group that had visited. We flew back home the next day. We went to Boston to touch the lives of those hurt in the bombing, to give them hope, but we ended up gaining so much back in return. When we left, our hearts were full of love, acceptance and peace.

In November of 2013, I got an unexpected call from Jason Castro's manager. They had seen my video circulating on YouTube (I had 40,000 views by this point) and asked if I would like to perform" Only a Mountain" with him.

"Heck, yes!" I shouted into the phone. "I've been wanting to sing with him since the day I put it on the Internet!" The closest stop on Jason's tour to my location was Andrew, Texas, so that's where I went to meet him.

On the day of the concert, I woke up in the early morning hours, drove for seven hours to get there, and went through sound check. I watched from backstage while he performed. Finally, I joined him for my part.

There had to be at least 1,500 people in the crowd, and I sang my heart out. Belting out the lyrics to that song with the guy who was a big part of the inspiration for me to get into music was one of the highlights of my life thus far.

Afterward, I got to hang out with Jason. He was just a normal guy who loves the Lord and music as much as I do. He said he was truly inspired by my story and was excited to have me perform with him that night. Singing with him opened up new doors for me.

IN JUNE OF 2014, I WAS GIFTED WITH A VACATION TO MAUI BY A new organization called Maui Warrior Appreciation Vacation. My friend Paul Volpe, whom I met when he visited the Center for the Intrepid, introduced me to the organization and traveled with me. Paul worked for an organization called Forward March that provided a program called Dancing with our Heroes for wounded soldiers in recovery. I took a few dancing classes from them.

I was so excited to be able to visit a place as beautiful as Maui! I managed to book an hour gig at a small music venue with a few local artists. My show was later in the evening, so we spent the day exploring.

We were out doing some sightseeing and as we passed a barber shop, for some reason Paul decided that this moment was the perfect time to get a haircut, so he popped inside.

I waited out front on a bench, but soon got bored. I had my guitar with me, so I took the opportunity to practice the songs I would be playing that evening. My fingers picked out the chords to "Fast Car" by Tracy Chapman. My voice rang out loud and clear.

Slowly, a crowd began to form. About fifteen people sat on the concrete around me, listening to me practice. Paul laughed when he came out from getting his haircut. "You sure know how to draw a crowd!" he smiled.

Someone shouted out, "Can you play any oldies?"

I smiled. "Well, I'm still learning, so not yet," I replied. "How about this?" I sang "Just the Way You Are" by Bruno Mars. I give it my all every time I sing. Why wouldn't I? The doctors plainly told me that I would never again speak clearly, let alone sing!

I love singing this particular Bruno Mars song because I really get to wail and work out my pipes. After I finished this song, my new audience clapped, and a man who had been sitting in the back of the crowd approached. He wore dirty, torn clothes. It didn't appear he had showered in a long while.

"Young man," he said, laying his hand on my arm, "your voice is angelic."

I wasn't about to argue with him, even though I disagreed, so I let him speak. He went on to say he felt the presence of God radiating through me. I have never felt as blessed as I did in that moment. I was accomplishing my goal.

I was playing random songs, and this man felt the spirit of God because of it. Situations similar to this have happened to me several times since then, and each time I feel it is a reminder from God.

It's like a little nudge from him to say, "See? I told you." All I had to do was listen.

* * *

IN JULY OF 2015, I MET STEVEN MARTIN AT GUITAR CENTER IN San Antonio. I was there checking out the equipment and heard him playing "Thinking Out Loud" by Ed Sheeran as I walked by a corner practice room. I went in, introduced myself, and asked if I could sing while he played. That led to a couple of hours of us jamming together.

A few days later, I joined him and his wife at a local venue for some live music, and then we hung out at my house after. We spent the evening playing guitar together and decided to try to book some gigs.

Our first show was at the 22nd Annual Balcones Heights Jazz Festival on August 7, 2015.

The crowd was warm, we played some great cover songs, and we longed for more. About a month later, Ron Grant, a friend that worked at Guitar Center, gave me the names of a few other musicians who might be interested in playing with us.

We formed a band called Company 6 with Eddie Keyz (keyboard), Rob (bass), Jae Hodges (drums), Steven Martin (guitar/vocalist), Gam Williams (keyboard/vocalist), Tim Martin (DJ/band manager), Trey (sub-instrumentalist), and me. Overall, we played about fifty official events together, but in 2018 God took each one of us on different paths, though each of us are still very passionate about our music.

I learned a lot about music, song writing and collaboration during this period in my life. I was ready for the next step in my musical career.

11

LEARNING TO SHARE MY STORY

Talking is a form of healing therapy. This is why so many people choose to see a therapist at some point in their lives. When overcoming a tragedy, it helps to talk about it, whether with a professional or just family or friends. We need to vent, to get our thoughts out there and to share with people who understand us.

As we go through life, we see people dealing with misfortunes and life disasters, and I have been no exception. I've watched my stepmom, siblings and friends all work through personal trials and tribulations. One thing all recoveries have in common is talking—and for many, laughing. If you can look back on your life as a whole, tell someone the story of who you were and how you became who you are today, and come away with a positive attitude and a smile on your face, you have accomplished quite a lot in my eyes.

Learning to smile and then laugh again doesn't always come easy. You've got to find the joy in your life. Joy from the flock of birds that you watched fly overhead. Joy from the nice stranger that just bought your Starbucks. Joy from being in the company of a good friend. And laughter is the evidence that joy has taken over in your life.

Laughter is medicine.

I will give props to modern medications and the healing power they can have on our bodies and minds, but the healing power of laughter is really something amazing. It has been proven time and time again. Studies have shown that laughter decreases stress hormones and increases our body's infection-fighting antibodies, which in turn stimulates our immune systems and helps to make us resistant to disease. When we have a good chuckle, our bodies release endorphins, the natural "feel-good" chemicals that travel to our brains and make us feel better. Endorphins give us an overall sense of well-being, and they have even been shown to be a temporary mechanism of pain relief.

Once you understand this, you can understand your own healing process. I realized that in the beginning when I was so completely devastated by what had happened to me and upset at God and the world, I was filling my body with negative thoughts and feelings that hindered me from healing.

Once I accepted what my new normal was, learned to love myself again, and *chose* to live with a smile on my face, I began healing physically, emotionally and spiritually.

I slowly started to share my story with others. I would show people pictures of what my truck looked like before and after the explosion.

Eventually, I could even share photos of what *I* looked like before and after the explosion. I didn't know if hearing about my experience would be helpful to others, but it certainly took a weight off my shoulders to get the story out of my head and vocalized to those that cared to listen.

I soon became accustomed to people staring at my legs or asking me what had happened. It no longer bothered me if kids pointed at me or flat out asked, "What's *wrong* with you?" Or, "Why are your legs metal?"

I could talk about it with anyone that wanted to listen and not feel an oppression on my spirit.

This is when I met Carolina.

After losing my legs and going through a divorce, I had begun to wonder what God had planned for me and if his plans included a relationship. I honestly thought no one would ever want to love me for me.

Carolina and I met via Facebook. I took a chance and chatted her up. She lived in Florida and seemed sweet and kind. We really hit it off. She had two cute kids—a boy and a girl. They were the nicest kids I'd ever been around, and I fell for them immediately. They understood what had happened to me and accepted my amputations and prosthetics.

The little girl, I'll call her "V," made quite an impression on me. She told me she was happy I had made it back home alive and thanked me for protecting our country. Then she hugged my legs. Her gesture was sweet and innocent.

The heart of a child is so pure and kind; I wish we all had that kind of attitude towards each other. I was beginning to feel that this might be the family God had set aside for me.

Carolina said she wanted to move to Texas to be with me, but the only thing stopping her was a little hiccup with her ex-husband in Florida. He was the father of her children, and when they were divorced, he won a court order that kept her from taking the kids out of Florida. She didn't have the finances to fight it, so she couldn't move her family to be with me in Texas.

I would have done anything to help her and the kids, so I offered her the money to take him back to court and she won. The court order was lifted, and she and the kids came to live with me in Texas when the school year ended. We had an amazing summer full of family outings and time to hang out. I grew closer to the kids each day and was loving my new little family. I asked her to marry me and she accepted!

As August approached, she and the kids went back to Florida to get ready for school to start. The plan was to let her daughter finish out elementary school with her friends before moving to Texas to be with me. The day she arrived back home, she called and told me we were finished.

What?! I was so confused and completely in shock. When she had left, I thought we were one big happy family, moving in the right direction. And now she was ending it after six months together? After all of the family dinners, and the times we had talked about our future and even agreeing to marry me?

It turns out that she had only wanted my money to get out from under her ex's thumb. I had helped finance her court battle, and now she was done with me.

I did the only thing I knew to do—pray for God to heal my broken heart. I prayed for peace, understanding and patience. Through prayer and meditation, I decided I needed to take a year for myself to learn and grow, and to not allow myself to jump into another potential relationship disaster.

So that's exactly what I did.

I focused on my music, I lived a normal life, and every day I came home to an empty house.

Day after day it was the same old routine. I'd walk through the front door to an empty space filled with complete silence. There was no one there to ask me about my day, no dogs leaping off the couch to come lick my hand, no squealing children running to give me a hug. I was alone.

JANUARY BROUGHT ANOTHER PRESIDENTIAL INAUGURATION THAT I was again asked to participate in. It was a quick trip, but relaxing. I performed a couple of songs onstage in the evening. President Trump shook my hand and personally thanked me for my service. He actually remembered me from our first meeting a month prior at his campaign in San Antonio when I had met him before he took the stage for his speech.

A Crystal-Clear Prayer

THE SPRING PASSED QUIETLY WITH GIGS AND SPEAKING engagements, but as the summer approached, the loneliness of the past year started to weigh on my heart.

I began praying for God to introduce me to my future wife. I didn't just pray for one in general, I got very specific.

"I want her to be kind, compassionate, loving and have a great smile," I started. "I want to meet her at the gym. I want her to have curly hair. I want her to be strong in her Christian faith. I want her to support me in my music career."

I felt it was important to include all the details I wanted in a woman. My thought was that if I prayed specifically in this way, I would know her when I saw her, and hopefully I wouldn't be unlucky in love any longer.

I spoke to God as I would a parent. I think he likes our prayers this way, like a continual conversation. I talk to him about my day, how I'm feeling, what I need. And he is always listening.

Shortly after this prayer, on July 12, 2017, I hit Gold's Gym at an unusual time for me. I always go twice a day, once at 9:00 a.m. and once at 6:00 p.m. My schedule never varies, but for some reason on this particular day, I went early in the afternoon.

I started my normal workout routine, beginning with my stretches first. I heard an infectious laugh to my right. I turned to look, and my eye was caught by a beautiful woman and her friend, working their triceps on the cable pull-down machine.

I find the triceps to be a challenging muscle group, yet one of my favorites to work on, so I thought I could work this into a conversation.

I know, I know. I'd been out of the dating scene for quite a while, and I needed to work on my pickup lines. But this was my shot. I strolled over to them casually and introduced myself.

"Hey, my name is JP," I started, holding out my hand.

"Hi, I'm Crystal and this is my cousin, Nicole," the beautiful woman answered back as we shook hands.

"I just wanted to say that you both are using that machine more properly than any of the guys I've ever seen here. Good job."

I gave the most charming smile in my arsenal and hoped for the best. Fortunately, it worked! That one compliment would change the entire future of my life.

I would later learn that Crystal was there serendipitously. She had come to San Antonio to audition for the San Antonio Spurs Silver Dancers, the dance squad for the basketball team. She made the initial cut but was let go right before the finals. She was ready to head back home, but her cousins, Zeke and Nicole, who lived in San Antonio, convinced her to stay and hang out with them for a few more days.

One of those days was when she walked into my gym. It was love at first sight for both of us. Numbers were exchanged, texts were sent, phone calls were made, Facebook requests accepted, video chats scheduled, girlfriend and boyfriend titles proclaimed.

She put in a job transfer to be closer to me, unpacked her luggage and, seven months later, said YES to becoming Mrs. Lane. When God has a plan, it can sometimes happen quickly.

On February 28, 2018, we went to the courthouse in Crystal's hometown of Brownsville, Texas and got married before a judge, family, friends and God. I knew she was the one God had chosen for me because of the way he placed her in my path at the right time. She has shown me nothing but love ever since. The best part about our small courthouse wedding was making sure Crystal's grandma and grandpa were there. This was the most important thing for Crystal and was even more of a blessing because the following year heaven gained a brave Marine. Her grandpa had been called home, but the pictures of him at our wedding will forever be with us.

We took our first big step toward a family by adding a Goldendoodle to our lives who we named Bentley. If it is in God's plan for us, we hope to have children running around our house one day.

As the days went by, we began forming a life together and started looking to what the future might hold for us. Crystal and I soon came up with an idea for a business venture.

When I had been in San Francisco for an American Idol audition, my dad and I took a walk around the bay. There were lots of shops and restaurants, and we spotted a custom t-shirt shop on one of the street corners. My dad thought it would be cool to get a shirt made to commemorate my time in Afghanistan. He suggested "Nice Try Afghanistan," but I corrected him by saying we were fighting against the Taliban, not Afghanistan itself. We ended up creating a t-shirt with

"Nice Try Taliban" emblazoned across the front of it. It only took about thirty minutes to print up and I wore it proudly to my audition.

When Hurricane Harvey hit the Texas coast in 2017, Crystal and I were intensely moved by the devastating images and saddening stories coming out of the aftermath. We wanted to do something to help—perhaps a fundraiser.

Crystal remembered my "Nice Try Taliban" shirt.

"What if we make that shirt again, but with 'Nice Try Harvey' on it instead? We could frame it with a big outline of the state of Texas!" she suggested.

We took our idea to Ibettink in San Antonio. The owner, Mrs. Shipley, wanted to help the victims as well, and she gave us the t-shirts at cost.

We asked the local Chick-Fil-A Manager, Mr. Ruben, if we could sell the shirts in his restaurant, and he happily agreed, even throwing in a free sandwich with every shirt purchase.

We wanted to give the money to an organization we knew and trusted, so we chose Adapt A Vet in San Antonio, Texas. They normally adapt homes for veterans but after the hurricane they were buying mobile homes and gifting them to veterans who were Harvey victims. Almost every weekend they were trucking in trailers full of furniture and home goods from San Antonio.

Crystal and I threw on our "Nice Try Harvey" shirts and made a weekend trip to meet some of the people in the area who had lost everything: houses, cars, various belongings, pets, their very livelihoods and their loved ones. Many were left with only the clothes on their backs.

It was painful to see the entire town still suffering so much a month after the hurricane had hit. Crystal and I did what we could, volunteering where Adapt A Vet needed us the most. I sang a song and told my personal story of moving past adversity with the desire that I would give them hope. I wanted them to know that this hurricane wouldn't stop them. It wouldn't ruin them.

They too would overcome.

* * *

CRYSTAL HAS BEEN SUCH A POSITIVE INFLUENCE ON MY LIFE, IN more ways than one. With her prompting, I now have a better relationship with my mother, the ability to embrace every opportunity to get my story out there, and this very book you are reading.

When Crystal and I first met, she had a great job working at BBVA Compass Bank. When we were married and became partners in this life, we also became partners in business. Managing my schedule had become almost a full-time job for me, and I struggled to balance the paperwork part with the fun part. I just wanted to get out there and play!

This is where Crystal stepped in and saved me. She is the Executive Director for JP's Journey. She sets up all my speaking engagements, handles all marketing projects and manages my social media accounts. So now *she* gets all the paperwork while I get to focus on music and doing what I can to help others.

I am blessed to have a wife who supports me and my choice of career. She works hard to get my story out there in hope of being able to inspire just one more person and is an integral part of our team. I know with her help we will reach the goal we set of inspiring a million people.

We've shared good times and hard times, and we work every day to point our relationship in the direction God wants us to be heading.

We've happily searched for those moments in life where we can clearly see God's intervention and handiwork.

Such was my meeting with a man named Lucas Cifka.

* * *

My Proper Exit

MANY PEOPLE BELIEVE THAT THERE CAN BE A "RIGHT PLACE AT the right time" moment or perhaps a person that might walk into your life when most needed. I like to call it a divine appointment—God set up this meeting.

I met Lucas when we moved into our neighborhood. We were both checking our mail at the same time and got to talking. He had also retired from the Army, and when he came over to visit, we'd chat about day trading stocks, new music or sports cars, just guy things.

One day in February of 2018, he hit me with the news that he had just gotten back from Afghanistan. No, he wasn't returning from active duty deployment, he was returning from closure.

You see, Lucas was a double amputee, just like me. He had lost both legs in a mission over in Afghanistan. Of course, I didn't know this at first and had no idea why he had gone back.

"Why did you go back to Afghanistan?" I asked, barely able to contain my shock.

"There is an organization that brings warriors back to where they were hurt, so they can get some sense of closure," he explained. "I went to go back over there and leave that country with pride. It's called Operation Proper Exit."

I was sold. I was completely unaware that there was such a group! I had been wishing for the means to do this on my own and here, standing right in front of me, was a man that God had clearly put in my path to give me just such an opportunity! This was my chance to finish my mission with my head held high.

The organization that runs Operation Proper Exit is Feherty's Troops First Foundation. Lucas gave me their contact information, and I called them that same evening. The phone rang. My heart was pounding harder than it had in a long time. Another ring.

"Troops First. This is Rick. How can I help you?" a baritone voice asked. I got right to the point.

"I am Specialist JP Lane," I said. "I was wondering if you have any more spots available for the next trip to Afghanistan?"

"Well, we've got a trip coming up in April. I think we may be full, but I can check tomorrow at our staff meeting," Rick stated. "But first, tell me about yourself. What's your story?"

I told Rick Kell, the co-founder of the foundation, the whole story: how I joined the Army and asked for the most dangerous job, how I had seen a friend paralyzed and another shot, how we had cleared Route Red Stripe once before in the day, missing one life-changing bomb.

I told him how I was blown up, how my foot was left in the truck, how I had countless life or death surgeries, how I got my sexy new legs, and how I had met Lucas who had given me his number.

Rick said, "I've heard of you before... you're a singer, right?"

"Yes, sir," I replied.

He paused. "All right. Let me see what I can do," he said. "I can't make any promises, but if I can't get you on this trip, you can join the next one."

I was beyond thrilled. "Okay, great," I replied. "Let me know what happens."

Two days later, my phone rang. It was Rick.

"JP, you're good to go. I got you in," he chirped. "Pack your bags. We leave in April."

I hung up the phone, my body buzzing with excitement. I just found out about this organization and here I am two days later with a ticket to Afghanistan! I was going to get to climb the biggest mountain in my life and plant a flag at the top.

As pumped up as I was, I knew my family wouldn't be quite as thrilled. In fact, most thought I had down-right lost my mind along with my legs. Afghanistan was still considered a war zone.

Crystal had known my plan all along. She had her reservations of course, but she was very supportive of my decision. Now it was time to tell her that it was official.

"Hey, sit down with me real quick," I said, directing her to the couch. "Rick called and he was able to get me on the next trip back to Afghanistan," I told her.

She squealed and hugged me. "That's great!" she exclaimed. "God has big plans for you in Afghanistan. You are doing exactly what he wants."

"You aren't worried? Or scared?" I asked her.

"Well, of course I am!" she answered. "But I am your wife, and I will always support you."

I called Anthony first, and then my dad.

"ARE YOU CRAZY?!" my dad shouted into the phone.

"Yes," I responded. "That's why I took the job in the first place."

He immediately asked a million questions about my protection and safety, and eventually I was able to convince him I would be okay. Even so, he questioned me every time we spoke, right up until the moment my plane took off.

"Is this really what you want to do?" he would ask.

"Yes, Dad. I want to do this, but I also *need* to do this."

I ran down my list of family and friends to call, and each conversation went basically the same. I would tell them my plan, they would express shock, fear and concern, and ultimately ask me if this was a good idea. Why would I want to go back to the country where my legs were taken from me?

"Yes, I know it's dangerous," I told each of them, "but I will have God with me."

I kept Psalm 23:4 close to my heart: "Even when I walk in the valley of darkness, I will fear no evil for You are with me."

If there was ever a "valley of darkness" for me, it was Afghanistan.

Time flew by and before I knew it, I was kissing Crystal goodbye. My dad flew in from Wisconsin to see me before I left. He gave me what may have been the biggest hug I'd ever had. I first flew to Washington, D.C. to meet the organization's leaders and the other veterans that were going on the trip. There were eight of us: one Marine, six Army soldiers, and one Navy sailor, ranging in age from twenty-nine to forty. Two of us were double amputees, a few were single amputees, and the rest had been shot or injured in other ways.

We made introductions, ate dinner together and spent some time getting to know our new brothers-in-arms. We were each given a brand-new uniform, which many of us had not been in since our injuries. The style and look had changed a bit from my time in the Army, but it felt good to put on my ACU's again. I ran my fingertips over the American flag and felt pride for my country. I glanced down and saw my name and rank stitched on my chest. I made sure my 428th Engineer Company patch was there.

Our flight was long, but it gave us time to swap stories. I chatted with Sergeant Hubert Gonzales, a single amputee from San Antonio. We spoke of our injuries and our families, what our lives had been like since we had been injured. It was good therapy. It was encouraging and enlightening to spend time with other guys in situations very similar to mine.

After multiple, incredibly long flights, we landed in Afghanistan. As we all took that first step off the plane, many of us were overcome with emotions. It was heartbreaking and heartwarming at the same time. I thought about the last time I had stepped off a plane into this war-torn country, my pack slung over my shoulder as I strutted into the desert heat, ready to take down the Taliban. This time was a completely different feeling, but nonetheless, I was still greeted with a hot, stiff wind full of gritty sand.

It was entirely surreal to be back in the country that took my legs from me, walking on two new legs, showing my unwavering strength and undying love for my country. Afghanistan *had not* and *would not* defeat me.

We traveled to four of the six bases in Afghanistan, including Jalalabad Airfield, Kandahar Airfield and Bagram Airfield, telling our stories and hopefully instilling hope and power in each life we encountered. Every base we visited welcomed us with great, truly patriotic, American fanfare. Our path into camp was lined for hundreds of feet with soldiers on either side. I walked down proudly bannering my "Nice Try Taliban" shirt. They clapped and cheered and saluted. Many shouted "Hooah" when we passed and reached out to shake our hands.

I couldn't imagine the Queen of England getting a warmer reception among her people than we did that day. We were all choking back tears, completely overcome by the emotions rattling through our bodies. The feeling of solidarity, of thanksgiving and of pride oozing off of every person there was almost too much to bear. The commanders rounded up the troops into a gym or large building, and the eight of us sat in chairs lined up in the front to tell our stories one by one. Everyone was given the chance to ask us questions. On one occasion Afghan soldiers came up to us and thanked us for our sacrifice. We felt a mixture of shock and gratitude toward their gesture.

At the bases, we shared laughter, tears and meals in the chow hall. During lunch one day, a contractor wove his way through the crowd, "Specialist Lane?" he called. "Specialist Lane?"

I stood up. "Here, sir!" I answered.

He approached me and shook my hand, putting his other hand on my shoulder as he spoke. "First of all, I wanted to let you know I appreciate your service and your sacrifice," he said. "I am very sorry for your loss. But I will say that you did not lose your legs in vain," he continued, "because the damage that IED caused to your truck, the way it passed through it, allowed us to research and develop a stronger vehicle design. We are using them now and to this day, not one has been penetrated. They are integral to winning this war."

Hearing this brought me to tears. Needless to say, I would have never known that if God hadn't given me the chance to go back.

Each base provided us with a specially planned activity. One of those was building a bomb. I couldn't have been more excited! Each warrior had the necessary tools and equipment to create one bomb. We all stood around each setup with our supplies and challenged each other to a timed completion. When mine was complete, I grabbed a marker and wrote "See if YOUR legs can take this!" It was a form of therapy knowing that I could get just a little ounce of payback with this bomb that was set to drop on a newly discovered cell of Taliban the next day. The Afghan Air Force was parked about 200 feet from us, waiting on their payloads.

When we first arrived in Afghanistan, I had mentioned to Sergeant Major Thomas Capelle, one of the leaders of Troops First, that I would like to sit in the driver's seat of a RG31 again.

I soon got my chance.

At the third base on our stop in Kandahar, we had a class on some of the new military equipment currently being implemented and used. I heard a familiar rumble of a truck engine and the sounds of tires crushing the dirt and rocks. I turned to look and saw an RG31 rolling straight up to my position—I couldn't believe it! I had been told there were only a few remaining in Afghanistan because they were being replaced with the stronger trucks able to withstand bigger IED blasts. ...and one had just pulled up right next to me like VIP valet.

I checked with the driver and he gave me the okay to climb in. With thrill surging through my veins, I climbed into the driver's seat, which was a challenge in my prosthetics. As it turns out, an RG31 is *not* handicap accessible. My hands gripped the wheel lightly and I put my prosthetic feet on the pedals. I looked in the rearview mirror. I checked the dials. In a weird way, it felt like I was home again, this familiar setting in which I used to spend a good portion of my days. I was thankful for the opportunity.

This time I *stepped* out of the truck, instead of being dragged out of it. It felt exhilarating. I called Crystal that night and told her all about my day. We were able to use a secure landline phone to communicate. She said she was praying for me every day.

As our trip was coming to an end, I felt like I had completed a huge accomplishment. I had done it! I didn't let the fear of the Taliban stop me. I didn't let doubtful people stop me. I didn't let my post-traumatic stress disorder stop me. I faced the very country that had tried to take me out of this world. I decided from that moment on that any PTSD I struggled with would stand for post-traumatic successful *domination*! No matter what might try to bring me down, with God's help I would dominate it!

We left wearing our military uniforms. This is the way I had imagined it the first time around, not strapped to a gurney tied up to IV drips and life-saving machines. I walked out of Afghanistan in my uniform, on my own two legs, with my head held high.

Better late than never. I had bottled up so much anger and frustration for all those years. Standing back in that barren desert allowed me to pull the last bandage off my emotional scars. And they had healed.

Goodbye Afghanistan. Goodbye hurt. Goodbye anger. Goodbye legs.

Hello America. Hello peace. Hello love. Hello prosthetics!

I finally felt complete and ready to show the world the new and improved JP Lane! Telling my story could have been an incredibly painful experience, but it is the most enjoyable thing I never thought I would do. I get to show wounded soldiers and hurting civilians alike that no matter what life throws at us, it's the mindset we approach it with that controls our direction. Positivity leads down a path of growth and change for the better. A negative attitude will send you down a dark and depressing road.

With God behind us, you can flip that switch from dark to light. You can decide to not let your traumas, trials and negative thoughts control who you are and who you could be.

In learning to tell my story, I have gained the confidence and support I needed to grow as a person. Sharing what happened to me has opened doors and lit pathways I never thought I would be traveling on. It has helped me become a better version of myself.

What will telling *your* story do for *you?*

12

WRECKS, CRUISES AND GAVIN DEGRAW

I couldn't wait to get home to Crystal and tell her all about my trip to Afghanistan. I filled her in on every single detail: about the amazing troops still over there serving our country, about the new trucks that the loss of my legs helped design, about the bomb I had made and about the lives that I hoped I had inspired.

We resumed life as normal and headed to the gym a few days later on a rainy Friday the 13th. After our workout, we grabbed some waters and headed home. We were about six miles from our house when a black Ford F-150 came around a corner, lost control on the slick roads and hydroplaned towards us. I quickly reacted and swerved our Jeep into the grass on the right shoulder to avoid him, but he still smashed into us. We flipped and rolled over twice. Air bags exploded into our faces. Our seatbelts held us in as we tossed and turned in the cab. The back glass shattered and sprayed all over the Jeep. We landed upright on the tires with a thud. Everything in the car had been tossed about and was in disarray. Later, we found Crystal's phone lying a few feet away in the grass.

Soldier mode took over. "Crystal!" I shouted. "Are you okay?"

"Yes," she replied, "I'm okay."

I could smell smoke. "Get out of the car, NOW," I commanded her.

She tried the handle. "I can't," came her reply. "The door is stuck."

I glanced over and saw that her door was completely crushed in. She kept trying, kicking with her feet.

"I'll get you out!" I promised her.

The smell of burning tires and locked brakes brought back memories of the blast in the RG31. I tried my door; it was smashed in as well. I punched it and threw my shoulder into it with all my might. It finally sprang free. I hobbled over to her side of the car. She had managed to wedge the door open about six or seven inches. I pulled on the frame and got it open enough that she could squeeze through. She fell to the ground on her hands and knees, barely conscious, panting and trying to gather herself.

I didn't see any blood; it didn't look like she had any broken bones. She was going to be okay. I held her in my arms. "You're okay," I reassured her, and myself.

"I love you. I love you," she kept repeating.

"I love you, too," I replied.

I thanked God for his protection, yet again.

The other driver came over to check on us. He was dazed from the crash, but otherwise okay. He was profusely apologetic and explained how the slippery road caused him to lose control on the curve. I worked to calm him down and let him know we were all okay.

"I think both our cars are totaled," he said, his hands on his head.

"Cars are replaceable," I told him. "The important thing is that we are all okay."

There wasn't even a broken bone among us. An ambulance took us to the hospital to get checked out. They wrapped Crystal in a neck brace, put her on a stretcher and hooked up an IV of fluids. The ride to the hospital gave me time to collect my thoughts. I couldn't believe what happened. I had *just* gotten back from my life-altering trip to Afghanistan, and here it seemed like the devil or the universe or *whatever* was trying to take me and my wife out. I wasn't gonna have that!

I cannot sing the praises of seat belts enough. Wearing them most certainly saved our lives. I called Anthony and he met us at Methodist Stone Oak Hospital in San Antonio. They were completely full but didn't turn us away. We were seen in the hallway outside the main Emergency Department. We both underwent MRIs and had X-rays.

Because of the projection of the collision, Crystal's head hit the passenger window, giving her a headache of massive proportions complete with muscle strains and nerve damage on the right side of her body. I luckily escaped with only muscle soreness and pain in my right arm. We were cleared to go home the same day.

Our friend Rox Contugno, the founder of Adapt A Vet, picked us up and drove us home. We were both incredibly sore for the next couple of weeks. Our wonderful neighbors brought us fully prepared meals, and Crystal's cousins brought us some much-appreciated Whataburger. On day five after the crash, the throbbing in my arm had grown unbearable. I went to BAMC to get it checked out. X-rays revealed internal bleeding where two metal plates had been placed to repair my arm following the blast in Afghanistan. The doctor said this new injury would heal on its own and gave me pain medication.

One week after the accident, we drove to Colorado for a gig. Fortunately, no motor vehicle accidents took place during that trip.

* * *

The Purple Heart Cruise

LATER THAT FALL, NOW FULLY RECOVERED, WE WERE INVITED TO go on a cruise. It all began one lazy afternoon while scrolling through Facebook and Crystal saw a post about the Purple Heart Cruise (PHC).

PHC is funded by a somewhat new organization that supports Purple Heart recipients and warriors wounded in combat. It started with one man's mission to give his wounded grandson a well-deserved vacation and morphed into a project that touches the lives of many soldiers and their families. We applied and were accepted!

Crystal and I were beyond thrilled to experience a cruise together, a first for each of us. We would be one of about twenty warriors and their families on board for the week-long cruise that would leave from New Orleans and travel to Montego Bay in Jamaica as well as to Grand Cayman Island and Cozumel, Mexico. Soon, our bags were packed; I grabbed my guitar and ukulele, and we headed for New Orleans.

Boarding the ship was an experience of its own. The enormity of the ship was like an airport, brimming with 3,000 people who were checking-in. It was just like TSA: they checked our tickets, passports, bags and persons. We were assigned a group and a time to enter. When it was finally our turn, everyone rushed to their rooms, excited to get their vacations started. The elevators were packed, and we had to wait for a while but finally made it to our room on the tenth level. Our names were posted on the door. Crystal and I gave each other big smiles and headed in.

We stepped inside and the first thing that grabbed our attention was the view: huge windows looked out over the rolling sea! Everyone was required to head to the auditorium for a safety briefing, and then those of us on the Purple Heart side met with the leaders and the other cruise recipients. We introduced ourselves and made fast friends.

Our days were filled with island excursions, sports competitions and more than enough activities to keep us busy. We spent the days at sea exploring the ship, eating way too much amazing food and meeting some incredible people. We took full advantage of the rooms reserved for us to pray and share stories.

Crystal and I love blackjack and spent some time in the huge casino. We found a table taking $5 bets, and Crystal turned her $60 into $320 in about an hour!

"I have taught my young padawan right," I chuckled to myself.

We watched a game called Love and Marriage. Cruise event leaders would choose three couples from the audience and ask them questions independent of one another, then they would guess what answers the other chose. There was a newlywed couple, one that had been married thirty years and an elderly couple that had been together seventy-two years. They were our favorites and knew each other so well.

Crystal and I played along and would whisper our answers to each other. Thankfully, I did pretty well!

One day consisted of a military appreciation event honoring all the veterans on board for their service. They called all military members and their families to the front of the ship in the auditorium. Each branch was announced and the men and women standing reported their names, their years served and their jobs. We shared a moment of silence for those who had given their lives serving our country. As I bowed my head, my thoughts drifted to Justin Ross and the outstanding example he had left for us all.

Inspired by the never-ending vastness of the sea and the awesome journeys of the people on board, I decided to write a couple of songs. As soon as I finished the first one, I asked the founder of PHC, J.J. O'Connor, and the cruise agent, Bob Bush, if I might have the opportunity to sing my song for any of those on board who wanted to listen.

We set up on stage and commandeered a microphone, and I sang my new song, "Gave It All Up," to a crowd of a few hundred people. I wanted to share with the Purple Heart veterans, who had sacrificed so much for our country, that God gave his only son for us. It was an amazing moment to be able to give glory to God for the sacrifice he made for us all.

Hanging out by the pool one sunny morning, we met new friends— Gio and Nany Feurtado. Gio was awarded the Purple Heart as well, and we all hit it off immediately. We hung out during the excursions and soon discovered that we live only two hours apart, which has allowed us to remain good friends and visit each other on occasion.

After a week of rest and relaxation, we headed back to real life filled with fun adventures and great memories. It was a special treat to be gifted with such a unique vacation. We were soon given the opportunity to cruise with the great PHC people again—Crystal and I were asked to join the 2019 5th Annual PHC, but this time as leaders!

We were more than happy to offer our services as workers this time around. We assisted part of the group, about eight service members, on the cruise with anything from locating their rooms, to setting up a time to play basketball, to finding the dining hall at the right time. We were their point of contact when they needed anything, but the most exciting part of our job was to inspire them and to offer a listening ear and friendly advice for healing and recovery.

* * *

Meeting Gavin DeGraw

In December of 2018, I was asked to perform at the Helping a Hero Lee Greenwood and Friends Concert in Houston, Texas.

The night before the concert I got a call from Meredith Iler, the President of The Strategic Alliance and leader of the Helping a Hero campaign. She asked if I was available to come sing and mentioned that Gavin DeGraw's manager would be there.

"What?!" I nearly shouted into phone. "Gavin DeGraw is performing?!"

"Yes," she replied. "He is scheduled to be the final performance."

I was definitely on board!

Several warriors, their family members, and Helping a Hero volunteers attended a VIP party at Topgolf in Katy, Texas where Meredith introduced me to Jeff Willett, Gavin DeGraw's manager. We talked about music for a while, and we found an opening in the conversation to ask if I could sing with Gavin.

At first Jeff was unsure, and I think he must have thought I was just this random guy at the event, but Meredith spoke up and explained that I was the beneficiary of a handicap-accessible home provided by Helping a Hero.

"He is a double amputee who lost his legs in Afghanistan," Meredith said to Jeff.

Now it made much more sense why I would ask to sing with Gavin at an event to benefit wounded veterans.

"Oh, my goodness!" he exclaimed. "I am talking to an American hero!" He took his hat off and shook my hand. He had no idea I was walking on prosthetics. Because he was so tall, he had no cause to look down at my legs and see them.

"You want to sing something for me now?" he asked.

"Sure!" I said, grabbing my little Martin guitar. I sang my go-to song, "Only a Mountain," and one I wrote myself called "Cruising With You" on my ukulele. He loved both.

After he left to pick up Gavin at the airport, I stayed and played a few more songs for the remaining guests. The next morning, I was on the CW News of Houston to speak about the event and share my story. The sound check was at two o'clock, and I spent the afternoon meeting and talking to some of the other acts that were to perform. Lee Greenwood was there, of course, as well as Scooter Brown Band and Tate Stevens.

Twenty minutes before the event doors were to open, I found Gavin on stage playing the piano and running through a final sound check. Jeff spotted me and waved me over.

"Hey Gavin, I want you to meet JP Lane," he said, introducing me. "He's a double amputee and a Purple Heart Veteran."

"Nice to meet you, man," Gavin said, shaking my hand. "Thank you for your service."

"I gotta say, I love your music." I gushed. "I even cover one of your songs."

"Oh, yeah?" he responded. "Which one."

"Not Over You," I replied.

The doors were opening in ten minutes. "You know what? Let me hear it," he said.

My heart leapt in my chest and my stomach flipped. "Absolutely," I said, trying to sound chill.

He sat back down at the piano and began to play. He started singing and I joined in right on cue. We finished the song and I caught my breath.

"Great voice," he commented.

"Thanks, man," I said, shaking his hand once again before I left for the green room to await my scheduled time. About thirty minutes later there was a knock on my door. I opened it to see Jeff, almost bouncing with excitement.

"You're not going to believe it!" he said excitedly. "Gavin asked if you would be interested in singing that song with him?"

I almost jumped for joy! "No way?" I cried. "Of course, I do!"

Jeff was almost as excited for me as I was. He told me he was almost in tears wanting to ask Gavin if I could sing with him, but he had wanted it to be Gavin's idea, so he knew it came from his heart.

I texted Crystal immediately and told her to get her phone ready to record the performance—I wanted to remember this forever! This was my Super Bowl moment!

My scheduled time slot came and went; I told my story, played and sang, then went backstage to rehearse a little more with Gavin. We worked out when I would come onstage and how it would all go. He showed great respect for the military and thanked me for my service.

When I finally took the stage with him, my heart was pounding in my chest and butterflies were flitting about in my stomach. The crowd was huge and welcoming as they cheered, shouted and sang along.

Singing with Gavin DeGraw was one of the highlights of my life. I walked off that stage feeling on top of the world.

13

THANK GOD I WAS BLOWN UP

Baby steps.

We think about taking baby steps in order to overcome life's little struggles: when we are actually learning to walk, or beginning to navigate through a career path, or getting back into the dating scene after a divorce.

Most people have only a few "baby step" periods in their lives. I have had more than most.

At age twenty-three, I literally had to go through baby steps again to learn to walk with prosthetics. But I say this next statement with one hundred percent sincerity: I thank God that I was blown up.

Yes, I know, that sounds crazy. I almost died; I almost left my family in mourning. I had to go through more surgeries than an average person can even dream of. I am missing parts of both legs and my right middle finger.

But my life now is a thousand times better, different and challenging than it was before. Sure, I'll never grow back my legs, and I know other issues will most certainly crop up from time to time, but I am a better person now.

I am closer to God, I am following his path for my life, and he has tasked me with inspiring and helping others—something I would have never dreamed I would be able to do.

I didn't write this book to fit in any particular category. It's not a religious book, but I love talking about the strength God has granted to me, and how he has changed my life.

This isn't a self-help book, but I will happily talk your ear off about how I was able to overcome my particular disaster.

It also isn't a book trying to garnish sympathy or attention. I do not feel sorry for myself and neither should you.

So then, what is this book? Well, I will tell you.

It is a powerful testimony to "Army Strong, God Strong." It's a story about the mountain that was put in the middle of my life, and my ability to overcome it. I am proud of what I have been able to accomplish thus far in my journey, and I'm looking forward to what I have yet to tackle.

I am most thankful for my family, my wife, my friends and my God. I am thankful for the love they have given me.

I pray this book has encouraged every reader to evaluate their own difficulties in life. Take a step back, look at those around you and the hardships they are struggling with, reassess your position in life, and then tell yourself, "You know what, I may have it bad, but not as bad as that guy did. If he can turn tragedy into triumph, so can I."

And I know you can.

Having said that, I do have one arch-nemesis: stairs.

I like to joke with people who have stairs in their homes that I will need one minute per stair to climb up. But do stairs hold me back? No. Do they deter me from my path? No. If I need to go up or down stairs, I get the job done. I may joke about it during the climb, but I won't let anything slow me down.

Occasionally, I will find myself climbing stairs in a foot race against an elderly gentleman or a baby learning to walk. It makes me chuckle every time; all of us struggling against the same task for different reasons, but all of us determined to win the battle. Half of the time, the man or baby will beat me, but when I finally make it to the top, I still feel like a winner.

This is a metaphor for life. It's climbing that mountain and making it move. We are always climbing, trying to better ourselves in everything we do. Sure, someone's probably going to beat us to the top, but we will beat others. When that happens, we can look back and extend a hand to help them finish the climb.

So many of us get upset when things don't go our way. We think God has turned his back on us or the universe is out to get us. How many times have we been disappointed because someone else got the promotion we thought we deserved? Or someone else got the new car or new house and we didn't? Or you feel you missed out on a blessing that you have been praying for over and over?

I've prayed to have my legs back; I wouldn't be human if I hadn't. I've prayed for God to turn back time.

But these prayers didn't stay on my list very long. I began to see that praying for the impossible like that would hinder the progress I wanted to make in my life. Certain prayers would restrict the impact of my story and even limit the blessing I would receive since my injuries.

I think of it this way: life is like a battery. If you look at the two terminals on the end of a nine-volt battery, you will find a negative and positive. The smaller terminal is the negative end.

I have had many small negatives in my life: the loss of limbs, the loss of a marriage, the loss of my memory and so many more.

We all have these types of losses, but we all too often focus on the negative.

However, if we look closely, sitting right next to the small, negative terminal of the battery is the larger, positive one.

We tend to look back at the past events of our lives and only see the negative. We need to take time to realize the positive. They often come packaged together, just like in a battery.

God gave me the time to recover and move forward in life, to advance my positive. It's easy to find God in the small things, things that seem to be designed by man, when you take the time to look.

If we can find him in the beautiful simplicity of something as mundane as a battery, we will be able to see him when the events of our lives take an unfavorable turn. The positive often comes out of the negative, or at least sits just opposite of it.

One of the basics of science that everyone is taught in high school is

Newton's Third Law of Physics which states that for every action, there is an equal and opposite reaction.

With this in the forefront of our minds, we can come to the conclusion that with every adverse event that takes place in our lives, a beneficial one has to be right around the corner heading our way. With God on our side, this positivity can end up being not just equal, but greater than anything negative that we have had to face.

We could learn a thing or two from the warriors that have been diagnosed with fatal diseases or illnesses that cripple the human body; yet, those warriors keep right on living life to the fullest. They don't dwell on their negatives; they live life! They spend time with their families, find organizations that raise funds for research, and even begin traveling the world to see as much as they can in whatever time they have left on this earth.

If we were to interview these people, I have no doubt that most, if not all of them, would tell us that they have more joy and satisfaction in their current lives than they ever did in the past. In the end, they will leave behind a wonderfully positive legacy, and those that remember them will do so fondly with love in their hearts and smiles on their faces.

These people are proof that life is like a nine-volt battery—but even more so, it's proof that God's love and grace is more powerful and amazing than we can ever fathom.

Every baby will eventually take that first step. They will grow older, stronger, wiser.

When I was learning to walk again, I was a baby in my prosthetics, but with each step I took, the same happened for me.

I grew older, of course, but most importantly I grew stronger and wiser, not just physically, but mentally and spiritually as well.

With every day that is given to us, we receive a blessing. We get another twenty-four hours, another 1,440 minutes, another 86,400 seconds to spend living our lives to the fullest.

Back in 2008, I signed the dotted line to serve and protect the American people. That was my oath.

I may not be wearing the uniform I donned after my enlistment, but that promise is still in my heart.

I am honored to serve at homeless shelters, to seek out those in need and bless them, and to travel to military bases to be an inspiration for those men and women currently serving.

It's always an amazing experience to visit schools and speak with kids facing adversity, or to take a positive mindset into our nation's prisons and talk with those who have made mistakes.

Though I am medically retired from the United States Army, I am still serving as a soldier in God's army.

Trust me when I say that *everything* happens in God's timing, not ours. It's okay if we don't understand things in the moment but remember that God always wants the best for you.

You naturally (even skeptically) might ask, "So, God thought you losing your legs was the best for you?"

I would answer you with a resounding "YES."

The old me wouldn't have been able to talk with others about their thoughts of suicide, to help people see past their struggles or to help those worse off than I am.

In fact, the old me would have *never* had the guts to stand up on stage in front of thousands and sing...but here we are.

* * *

SINCE I LAUNCHED MY MUSIC CAREER IN 2013, I HAVE HAD THE pleasure of playing with some of the greats, including Lee Greenwood, Aaron Tippin, Neal McCoy, The Gatlin Brothers, Gavin DeGraw and the man that started it all, Jason Castro.

I've been able to share the stage with many artists that I admire and aspire to be like one day. My hopes for the future are big: I would be thrilled to sing with some of my favorites like Justin Timberlake, Maroon 5 or Bruno Mars.

I cover songs by all of these great musicians and love the way their upbeat music puts a smile on your face or makes you want to dance. It's *that* energy and enjoyment that I strive to recreate when I play. If it's in God's plans to put me on a bigger stage, great, let's go! If he feels I am doing his best work where I am now, then that's just where I need to be.

I will always tell my story and do my best to inspire the crowd. Music isn't just about entertainment; it's about spreading a message.

That message can be love, hope, peace, inclusion, equality, power... anything! It is whatever you make it.

My message is one of hope and encouragement. I want to be able to reach out to that individual in the crowd that's having a really terrible day and maybe only ended up at my concert because a friend dragged them along.

I want to reach out to the person that's been living in despair and depression, maybe contemplating suicide. I want to find that guy or girl in the crowd that needs nothing more than to feel God's love in that moment. If I can ease their troubles, take their minds off the mountains in their lives, maybe even entertain them for a bit and let them know *it gets better*, that's all I can ask for.

Being on stage will always be a thrill for me. It's so much fun and it comes more naturally to me than I thought it ever would. When I am up there, playing my guitar and singing my songs, I don't even feel like I am wearing prosthetics.

I forget the blast.

I forget the surgeries.

I forget the pain, the suffering and the thoughts of suicide.

I forget my ex-wife.

I forget the Taliban.

All my past and present troubles fade away and...

I. JUST. PLAY.

I want to impact each and every person in that crowd with the mindset of dominating life's struggles, whether they are walking on their own two legs or in a couple of amazing prosthetics.

I hope I have inspired *you*.

EPILOGUE

I've watched, listened and prayed over the years and have seen the complete transformation JP has gone through. From being pulled—bloodied and bruised—from that truck to the walking, talking, and *singing* man he is now. He is doing remarkably well.

While he is not helping directly with my non-profit organization, he is a huge help indirectly by performing benefit concerts for us. He decided to pursue his true passion: music. He has brought joy and inspiration to my children, my wife and me during the three cross-country trips we have made to visit him.

He is a remarkable young man whose strength and resiliency are a blessing to others. He has chosen to turn his tragedy into a triumph.

— *SK Alfstad*

ABOUT THE PUBLISHER, TACTICAL16

The victor always writes the history, but oftentimes that history is written by someone that neither served nor lived during the conflict. Tactical 16 is on a mission to write the history of America's conflicts by those who experienced them—all of it, the messy and chaotic, and the tragic, the stories of good people in dangerous situations and the wrong people that made conditions perilous, as well as the politics and policies that impacted organizations at a fundamental level for better or worse.

Aside from helping to preserve history and assisting those with PTSD during the writing process, Tactical 16 has published books in children's, business, leadership, and fiction genres. They continue to look for those unique stories that are uncommonly told by civilians, veterans and first responders young and old.

The name Tactical 16 has two parts. Tactical refers to the armed forces, police, fire and rescue communities. The "16" is the number of acres destroyed on September 11, 2001, at Ground Zero.

Made in the USA
Las Vegas, NV
14 November 2021

34426077R00085